I think of the many teenagers and young adult women in my local body church who feel unloved, and they need to read and absorb *Invisible*. Jennifer writes simply, delightfully, and to the point about your value as a person.

—Pam B.

By the first few pages of chapter 1, I wanted to scream, "That's me!" Jennifer's storytelling is so personal, like sitting down over tea with an old friend and chatting. Reading this book reminded me that Christ sees me as His beloved, and it made me feel ten feet tall and proud to be Christ's precious child!

— Kim L.

Jokingly, friends and I say we are more tempted to run away from home as adults than we were as children! The chaos of work, children, ministry, and responsibility leads my heart to wander and ask, "Is this it? Is this all I am?" Jennifer helped me understand that downward spiral of questioning and doubting and how it all gets back to our Source of identity.

—Kristin H.

I have often felt like a "Gomer" and can relate to feeling "invisible." I am a single woman who has always longed for that special man, and haven't always made the best choices when it comes to relationships. Now as a woman who has accepted Christ, I still find relationships with men hard, and I tend to shy away for fear of rejection. I know I am loved completely by the Father, and I truly needed the reminder that He accepts me just as I am and expects no more from me than to be who He has created and is creating me to be.

—Jackie F.

Confession time! I am a fake! I have stared at, ignored, and judged many "Gomers" in church, work, and the marketplace! Did I act as Hosea did toward Gomer? No...I bypassed them, leaning toward "pretty people" …people who appeared "fixed"! Today, I am on my knees asking forgiveness...and for grace to become more like Hosea...

—Bettie B.

At a time when insecurity and invisibility mark my life, the teachings and questions in this book shot straight to my core, disengaging the cloak that Satan was attaching to me. Who knew I was a Gomer girl?

—Cynthia M.

I'll be honest — I never thought I could relate to Gomer. But in the opening pages of *Invisible*, Jennifer Rothschild reminds us that we are Gomer when we go looking for love, acceptance, and OURSELVES anywhere other than God. We are all Gomer girls, and, just like Gomer, we need to remember that we are God's beloved.

—Melody N.

Somewhere along life's journey, now at age 70, I lost my spiritual identity. The path back to healthy spiritual self-esteem is laid out plainly by Jennifer (and supported by God's Word) in this book.

—Judith M.

I laughed, cried, and thought about myself and my relationship with God. I love how Jennifer presents stories in such a vivid and real way. Throughout the book, there are so many profound statements that shook my heart to make me move a step further in my daily walk.

—Yolanda B.

As I read this book, God spoke to my heart that my identity is in Him. For years it was in my work, then in my Mom. I have wondered, "Who am I?" As I read, I felt alive again. As I read "God is always ready to redeem you to rest in His abundant grace," I felt a burden lifted.

—Karen G.

INVISIBLE

JENNIFER ROTHSCHILD

HARVEST HOUSE PUBLISHERS
EUGENE, OREGON

Cover photos © Jo Ann Snover, Iryna Rasko / Shutterstock; DonNichols / iStock

Cover by Harvest House Publishers Inc., Eugene, Oregon

INVISIBLE

Copyright © 2015 by Jennifer Rothschild
Published by Harvest House Publishers
Eugene, Oregon 97402
www.harvesthousepublishers.com

Library of Congress Cataloging-in-Publication Data
    Rothschild, Jennifer, 1963-
    Invisible / Jennifer Rothschild.
      pages cm
    ISBN 978-0-7369-6573-6 (pbk.)
    ISBN 978-0-7369-6574-3 (eBook)
    1. Bible. Hosea—Criticism, interpretation, etc. 2. God (Christianity)—Love—Biblical teaching.
    I. Title.
    BS1565.52.R68 2015
    224'.606—dc23

                               2015007408

Contents

Acknowledgments

With heartfelt thanks...

To Phil: There are just not enough pages in this book to capture all I could say about who you are and what you do! You are both my coach and cheerleader, and I am forever grateful for how you sacrifice for me and the ministry God has given. I couldn't do any of this ministry thing without your guidance and enthusiasm—and, I wouldn't want to either.

To Connor: You're the only child still home, and you're so flexible and patient with your mom's weird hours! Thank you, son. You make me laugh and think—I'm so proud of the man you are becoming.

To Clayton and Caroline: Even though you live far away, you are always so close to my heart. Thank you for all of the texts that encourage me and make me smile. I am so proud of you both.

To Harvest House: So glad I'm home! Thank you for your consistent and unwavering commitment to Jesus and for your patience and kindness toward me.

To Leslie, Valerie, Carolyn, Nicole, Terrie, Denise, Teresa, and Pat: You all work so hard to make everything look easy! You are true partners in ministry, and I thank Father God He has brought us together.

To Paula and Joan: What would I do without you? God used you in more ways than I can list to help me along the way. Thank you for the homemade bread, the lake rescue, the laughter, the prayers, the tears, and the endless supply of Tasia! I am so thankful for your faithfulness to God and for your friendship to me.

To Drew Voris: Just because you keep hounding me about your name appearing in one of my books! There, Drew, satisfied? Keep growing in your faith, little brother, God has a bright future for you.

The ME in GoMEr

One humid August day, my husband, Phil, and I flew down the highway in our ultracool white minivan. (We call it the "swagger wagon"!) We were in a huge hurry because it was just the two of us on our way to a much-anticipated lakeside getaway. To help pass the miles, Phil turned on satellite radio—you know the one with about three thousand channels? He began with the audio feed of ESPN sports, which I quickly tuned out. He then flipped over to an afternoon talk show, and I spent the next part of our journey doing my best to ignore the host, guests, and audience members yelling at—as well as over—each other.

Next, he tried a live audio feed of one of the major news outlets. Listening, I mused that most of the news we were hearing couldn't really be classified as news at all. These 24-hour stations had a lot of time to fill, and the stories reflected that fact. They were shallow and irrelevant.

How was I to know how relevant they would become for me?

While listening to all this chatter, I was bombarded with about three hours' worth of commercials—more than a lifetime's worth in my opinion! By the time we arrived at the lake, I was frustrated by the sad state of our media. I was concerned about the future of our country. But the main thing—the most important thing—on my mind was *me*.

Are my teeth white enough? How do I get rid of my hard-to-lose belly fat? Do I need to take fish oil?

I sized myself up by comparing myself to that brilliant news anchor I had just listened to and determined she was definitely smarter than me—and probably thinner too! *I bet she takes the fish oil I should probably be swallowing for my aging brain.*

All of a sudden, I was uncomfortable with everything about me—things I hadn't even thought about before—because I hadn't spent this much time in a long time focusing on *me*.

Was I skinny enough? Cute enough? Successful enough? Was my skin too wrinkly for my age? Did I need an eyebrow lift? Could that berry extract booster for only $30 a month really make me trim, give me more energy, and totally change my life?

And what about my thighs? According to one of those talk shows I'd just heard, my thighs were definitely too flabby. I poked and pinched them as Phil drove along, and by the time we got to the lake, I was convinced that not only were my thighs too flabby, but I also needed a knee lift. Yes, I had just learned from satellite radio that women get them, and I wanted one. No, I needed one! Badly!

When we arrived at the lake, I pulled the seatbelt from my hard-to-lose belly fat and swung my thunder thighs out the van door. As the skin under my eyebrows and above my knees simultaneously sagged to my ankles, I lumbered into the condo.

You'd think that by then I would be more than ready to shift the focus off of me and instead just relax at the lake, right? Not a chance! As soon as I'd brought in my luggage and settled in, I fired up my Facebook and Twitter iPhone apps to write a post.

As I leaned back in the creaky bamboo rocker on the deck and turned on Twitter, I was notified that someone had retweeted me. For you non-Twittery people, this means that a follower quotes something you tweeted and sends it out to their followers.

Most of the time, I barely notice. I rarely click on the link to find out what else they may have retweeted. But this time—with my mind totally on me, myself, and *oh, my!*—I felt the need to see who else my follower had retweeted.

So I started scrolling. And you know what I discovered? I am not nearly as clever as that brilliant woman whose tweets are so profound. I have far fewer followers, so I must not be as interesting or well liked. I am obviously not as capable and keen because I can manage tweeting just once or twice every two days, but other friends of mine seem to tweet up to 12 times a day. (I know this because I counted. Yes, can you believe I counted?) And they are so much wittier! How can they be that funny using so few letters? They have a presence on Pinterest. You can find them illuminating Instagram. They're brilliant and busy, put-together and perfect. How perfect? Most of these women I was comparing myself to blog every day. E-V-E-R-Y-D-A-Y! Seriously, sometimes I don't even shower every day. That's not something I would tweet (#gross).

All Twitter was doing was making me feel insecure. So what did I do? I closed Twitter...and opened up Facebook. And instead of popping open my page and leaving a post, I clicked on the pages of other friends—especially the other authors and speakers I know.

Now, here's something you need to understand. Because I am blind, navigating Facebook is just plain hard for me. Even though my iPhone talks to me, Facebook isn't always user-friendly for those who can't see. So for me to spend my time—precious time that I should have spent refreshing and recharging—clicking and tapping until my knuckles were swollen and my fingertips were raw just shows my momentary obsession with myself and my desperate search for a sense of identity. In comparing myself to these other women, I found myself falling short in just about every category.

I wasn't popular enough. My posts weren't pithy enough. I needed to engage my audience more. Showing my vulnerability? I wasn't doing that either. (I discovered that followers light up the "like" button when the poster seems frail, authentic, or vulnerable.) And as far as friends go—well, I was hundreds of followers behind this woman or that woman!

Here I was measuring my success by how many Facebook followers I had. Whatever the number, it was lower than hers, so it wasn't high enough. My level of self-awareness was at an all-time high, and my sense of value was at an all-time low. By this point, I was completely discouraged and feeling like an uninteresting, droopy-eyebrowed, saggy-kneed, unpopular, has-been woman.

Compared to everyone else, I felt invisible.

I hadn't thought about myself this much for this long in years, and I was miserable. The more I looked at me to find me, the less I could see who I was.

Now, you may think that someone like me who is often in the spotlight has no reason to be so whiny! I know, I know. I'm not proud of what I just shared with you. You may also think I would—or should—never feel this type of insecurity. You may wonder how someone who is seen and heard by so many people could ever feel insecure, inadequate, or invisible. But I want to be gut-honest with you right here at the start of this book. Sometimes the spotlight can accent, point out, and advertise every insecurity you have—even insecurities you didn't know you had! And the more people you have staring at you, the more invisible you can feel. We are all the same, whether we stand in the spotlight or feel like we live in the shadows. We all long to be seen, known, and accepted.

Now, I could explain my momentary identity crisis by saying, *See what media will do to a woman?* I could recommend we all turn off the television, retire the radio, and stay off social media. I could suggest that we eliminate all forms of advertising from our lives and thus avoid those evil marketers whose goal is to make you feel like a loser so you will purchase their products. I could rant and rave that Facebook and Twitter will do nothing but pulverize your self-esteem. But media isn't the problem. Media simply reveals the problem.

On that August day, the media merely served as a spotlight shining on the issue that was already there. I was having a walking, talking, Facebook-stalking identity crisis!

But wait a minute. How could this happen? After all, I was a Christian, for heaven's sake! I knew that God loved me and that I was valuable to Him no matter how many Facebook friends I had. I also knew that my identity was in Christ. So how could an identity crisis hit me—and hit me hard? My identity was in Him, right? But why didn't that *feel* right?

Isn't who I am based on who He is? And if it is, then why was I trying to find myself?

If I really believed that God sees me, why did I feel invisible?

If I am in Christ, why am I in crisis?

I know why—it's because I am prone to wander.

I am always one errant thought away from rejecting the truth that God accepts me and, instead, adopting the lie that He accepts everyone *except* me. I am bent on turning toward myself to find myself, gazing into my own eyes to find my identity, and basing who I am on how I feel.

It's my human nature. It's all of our natures. Like everyone else on planet Earth, I am prone to wander. I am bent on turning toward myself, being the first and biggest thing on my mind, obsessing about me, myself, and I—and straying from God.

What about you? Have you found yourself wondering why you don't measure up to your own—or somebody else's—ideals? Have you wasted time comparing yourself to others? Have you looked in the mirror and thought, *I'll never be good enough*?

As you consider your answers, I'd like to introduce you to a woman who had an identity crisis of biblical proportions. Loved beyond belief, this woman should have been able to rest secure in her identity. But she made the fatal mistake of wondering...and then she started wandering.

"Hosear" and "Goma"

I first heard this story from my dad, who was a master story-teller. Growing up, I loved the way he wove together tales that blended a lot of God's truth, a little bit of imagination, and a whole lot of Southern drawl! In fact, sometimes I couldn't quite make out the characters' names because they were lost in Dad's sweet, slow Southern twang. When he told me the story I'm about to tell you—a love story about a very unlikely couple—I honestly thought the characters were named "Hosear" and "Goma"! As far as I was concerned, those were their real names until I realized years later that not everyone talked with my dad's "Jimmy Carter" accent.

Hosea (not Hosear!) was a young preacher—a prophet, really—who lived at a time when religious people weren't interested in hearing his message. Instead of listening to God, the Israelites were more interested in living life on their own terms. (Sound familiar?) They were, as the hymn goes, "Prone to wander...prone to leave the God I love."

Then, one day, God surprised Hosea with a memorable message: Hosea's bachelor days were up! But the good news came with some bad news. Yes, Hosea would get married to a beautiful woman named Gomer (not Goma!), whom he loved. But his wife would break his heart. She would love him and leave him—leave him betrayed, bewildered, and brokenhearted.

Yet this would not be the end of the story. Not by a long shot! God would help Hosea pick himself up, dust himself off, and then do the unthinkable—bring his wandering wife back home. And he'd actually have to pay money to get her back. He would have to redeem her.

At this point, Hosea must have cried out to God, "Redeem my wife? She's thrown my love away! Why should I have to buy back what is already mine?"

But he did. Hosea walked up to the slave block and saved the unfaithful Gomer, proving that love can overcome that which seems lost forever.

His love overcomes that
which seems lost forever.

The story of Hosea and Gomer is a love story from ancient times. It's also the story of God's love for Israel. But beyond that, did you know that it's also your story and my story? It's a story about finding your identity in the perfect love of God, returning to the truth of who you are, and finding out that you are never invisible. You *do* matter.

Prone to wander, Gomer was bent on turning from her husband's love. So she set out in search of something more in her life—something more exciting, more gratifying, more daring. Hosea's love should have satisfied her, but a combination of factors—the culture of the time, Gomer's own family background, and her human tendencies—put her on the dangerous path of considering only herself.

The book of Hosea uses some strong words to describe Gomer's—and Israel's—tendency to turn away. Get ready—this could be harsh! The Bible uses words like *adulterer*, *harlot*, and *prostitute*. Ugly, right? I'd never want to be called any of those names. Would you? I'm sure that even Gomer wouldn't want any of those words describing her on her Facebook profile—even if some of the men of her time "liked" her status! No way!

Because I don't like those words—and because I feel so far removed from them—it's easy for me to keep Gomer at arm's length. I can view her from the tippy-top of my ivory tower, shake my head, point my finger, and murmur, "Tsk, tsk, Gomer." I can refuse to identify with her at all and cop an attitude that communicates I would never do that, so I could never be her.

But I have more in common with Gomer than I might think. In fact, we all have something in common with her.

So instead of labeling Gomer and distancing ourselves from her questionable past and lousy choices, let's look at the root of her problem to see if we can better identify with it—and with her.

Prone to Wander

In Hosea 11:7, God sums up the wayward or adulterous tendency—Gomer's, Israel's, and ours—with one statement: "My people are determined to turn from me."

Now, you probably wouldn't identify yourself as a harlot or an adulterer, but do you consider yourself "prone to wander"? You may have had a much better upbringing than Gomer had or made better life choices than she did, but what about your tendency to wander away from your true identity in the Lord and search for your identity elsewhere—like I did at the lake when I found myself Facebook stalking?

So, how prone to wander *are* you? Let's do a little exercise to find out. Grab a pen and, on the scale below, circle how prone you think you are to wander away from God.

(Not at all) 1 2 3 4 5 6 7 8 9 10 (Extremely)

If you marked anything below 5, let me clue you in to something you may not really understand about yourself and your Gomer tendencies. The prophet Isaiah (who, by the way, served the Southern Kingdom of Judah at the same time Hosea served the

Northern Kingdom of Israel) will tell you for me. Isaiah 53:6 says, "We all, like sheep, have gone astray, each of us has turned to our own way." Like sheep, we all have a tendency to wander and turn away. Really, all of us should circle 10 on the prone-to-wander scale!

I honestly didn't think I was a 10. After all, I had never left God, renounced my faith, or done anything so radical as to make it appear that I had turned away. But I finally realized where I stood on that August day at the lake. Maybe my mouth preached that I believed. Maybe my written words showed my strong faith. But in reality, my heart had strayed. I was looking for validation outside of God. I was determined to be somebody—as modern-day culture defines *somebody*. I was trying to find myself in all the wrong places, just like Gomer.

Of course, Gomer's actions weren't my actions, and they probably aren't yours either. But wandering from God doesn't have to happen on the grand Gomer scale for it to be real and dangerous. We begin to wander when we look away from God and look to others for approval. We start to stray when we are tempted to search for something that gives us a bigger buzz than God does. That's what I was doing on my iPhone that August day.

When our thoughts wander from God, we begin to wonder who we are. And when we wonder who we are, our actions will start to wander. We'll venture farther from God to find out who we are. We'll head away from Him and pursue other people and places, seeking our identity. And that's when we find ourselves feeling totally invisible—right in the middle of an identity crisis.

> When we leave our Source of self, we lose our sense of self.

Isn't it refreshing to know that you're not the only one who struggles with your identity? As we look at Gomer's life and consider our own, please join me in thinking through these questions:

- What is my identity?
- What is my identity based on?
- Do I identify with my identity?
- Do I accept myself?
- Do I think God accepts me?
- Do I feel invisible?

From Identity Crisis to Identity in Christ

There is a "me" in GoMEr—and there is a "you" in Gomer too. It's the part in all of us that is prone to wander and stray from God. It's the part in all of us that loses our God-given identity as we search for who we are in the world and forget about God. The funny thing is when we forget God, we can't remember who we are.

Like Gomer, we wander off to other lovers of acceptance, significance, and approval because we aren't secure in our identity.

When we don't accept who we are in Christ, we seek acceptance from those "other lovers" to discover or validate who we are.

And our culture—like Gomer's—makes it easy for us to do this. All we need to start the downward spiral is to compare our "likes" to someone else's.

Oh, girl, just like Gomer, many women don't live like God's beloved. We don't internalize that His love has made us lovely. We don't rest in the reality that His sufficiency has made us good enough. We don't identify with our identity. We don't accept that God has accepted us.

We're often quick to see our own weaknesses and flaws. But we're also quick to overlook what God sees in us. What God sees in us is what Hosea saw in Gomer, but she didn't see it in herself, and that's part of the reason she felt invisible and wandered. And my guess is it's part of the reason we wander too.

> When we don't see
> the truth that we are loved,
> we seek proof that we are loved.

God chose you and me as His beloved. And when we, like Gomer, turn away from Him and proceed down the path of wandering, He is always ready for us to return to Him, to regain our rightful identity as His beloved.

I've been Gomer, confused and stuck in chains of insecurity that I thought would certainly choke me. I've stood in her shoes, unable to free myself—unable, really, to even like myself. But God didn't just see where I was—He saw who I was, and He sees who you are too. You are never invisible to Him.

Have you been striving for acceptance? God can free you to accept who you truly are.

Have you been stuck in an identity crisis? God can reveal your real identity—one that you can smile at.

Have you felt overlooked, inadequate, or invisible? God can show you once and for all that how you feel is not who you are!

Oh, girl, are you ready to come with me on this journey?

I promise you I'll walk with you through every page of this book so you can get to a place where your feelings won't dictate your identity, your past won't determine your future, and lies won't dominate your thinking.

We can get there—or stumble there—together!

Instead of constantly striving for acceptance, you will be free to accept the you that God accepts. Instead of being perpetually stuck in an identity crisis, you will rediscover your worth. Instead of feeling overlooked or undervalued, you will discover that you have never, ever—no, not ever—been invisible to God.

Who I am

is found in

who He is

#TheInvisibleBook

The Wedding

*When the LORD first spoke through
Hosea, the LORD said to Hosea, "Go, take
to yourself a wife of harlotry and have
children of harlotry; for the land commits
flagrant harlotry, forsaking the LORD."*

HOSEA 1:2 NASB

She greeted me as I entered the cafeteria on Parents' Day. Our oldest son, Clayton, was a freshman at Baylor University, and this was the first time after dropping him off at college that we'd been back to visit. We had met faculty members, the resident director of his dorm, and lots of his new friends. So when this woman greeted me, I politely asked, "Now, tell me who you are?"

The woman hesitated. Her pause made me wonder if I had said something wrong. Maybe she wasn't accustomed to being asked this question. *Maybe*, I thought, *I should know who she is.* I imagine she looked down and saw my white cane and realized I couldn't see her, and that may be why she answered in a warm voice, "Oh, ma'am, I'm nobody. I just clean tables."

I reached toward her and found her hand. "You are not a nobody! You are not *just* a table cleaner!" I told her. "My name is Jennifer. What's yours?" She laughed and told me her name. As I told her goodbye and walked with my son to our table, I thought, *Nobody is a nobody!*

And it's true, isn't it? Nobody is a nobody, and nobody is *just* a table cleaner. Or *just* a mom. Or *just* a clerk. Or *just* an...anything! But we often find ourselves in places or seasons of life where we feel like a nobody. It can be hard to see our own value if we are feeling constantly overlooked or we associate our value with our virtue. You know, if we are good, we are worthy of being acknowledged. If we behave, we merit attention.

I have a feeling that our girl Gomer might have felt that way. After all, if she'd been asked, "Tell me who are you?" she'd probably say, "Oh, I'm nobody."

But her answer should have been, "I am Gomer."

I know, I know—what a name! Not pretty, but I bet she was.

She lived in the Northern Kingdom of Israel in the mid-800s BC. All we know about her is written in the book of Hosea, and when the book opens, she is a single gal! I imagine, though, that she doesn't lack for dates. She's never home on the weekends, and she apparently has quite a reputation. Her dresses are a little tight, her skirts somewhat short, and her blouses a bit low. Let's just say that men really enjoy her company.

We don't know tons about Gomer, but we do know that her father's name was Diblaim (Hosea 1:3). Like many biblical names, the meaning of her father's name is significant. It means "double portion of raisin cakes." Now, raisin cakes were like an aphrodisiac in Gomer's time. So Diblaim's name implied a lot about his character. It's safe to say that he probably lived up to his name. He was likely so into his own lust that he valued his own satisfaction more than he valued his daughter. So it could be that the only time Gomer got attention from her father was when...Well, you can imagine. I'm guessing she saw much more than a little girl should see. Her innocence was probably stolen from her and replaced with a knowing that no girl should have. Likely Gomer was a teenager whose innocence was so far in her rearview mirror that she couldn't even remember it.

So what's a girl to do? She either withers up in shame or fear, or she just goes with it. Gomer went with it—and became quite a mess. She partied and went for men who reinforced what she thought of herself. To get attention from a man—even the wrong kind of man—was what she wanted, and she did whatever it took to get that attention. She got around and had quite the reputation. She wasn't the kind of woman a man wanted to marry. She was the kind of woman a man wanted to...Well, use your imagination. Let's just say that Gomer was known as easy and available. There were whispers around Israel that she was actually a prostitute.

Gomer was probably stuck in painful self-awareness, lost in insecurity, and longing to be accepted for who she was, not for what she could do. Her shaky upbringing probably was part of the reason she made the choices she did when she grew up. Of course, I'm using my imagination based on a few facts from Scripture because all we really know of her family is the name of her father and the lifestyle she lived as an adult. But names meant something in the Bible, so dear old Dad's name represented who he was. And Gomer's name? It meant "completion," as in the filling up of the measure of idolatry or fully-ripened wickedness. From her name we can gather that Gomer's lifestyle was the fully-ripened effect of her father's selfish and sinful choices.

The Bible doesn't say anything about Gomer's mother. But because she is silent in Scripture, let's have her be silent in this story too. I suppose she might have been one of those mothers who acted like nothing wrong or inappropriate was going on. Gomer probably didn't know if it was powerlessness, denial, ignorance, or apathy, but her mom may as well have been absent. As a grown-up, though, I bet Gomer understood her mother a little better. She was as enslaved as Gomer was—just for different reasons.

Overlooked and undervalued, Gomer likely felt unworthy—like a nobody.

Now, here's where the story gets really interesting. Even though she saw herself as invisible, as least likely to stand out in a good way, Hosea saw her. And he chose her.

Who, Me?

It's really hard to imagine Hosea—a preacher, a prophet—marrying a woman like Gomer. That just doesn't happen! And because it's so beyond our realm of imagination, we could dismiss it as simply something cultural and miss out on the power of this story. So let's yank Gomer's story out of history and bring it into our own backyard.

Think of the most godly, spiritual man you can imagine. He's charming, handsome, and...single! Pretend he ministers at a church. How about your church? Hey, let's make him your pastor—your single, most-eligible-bachelor pastor! People listen to him Sunday after Sunday as he teaches God's Word. All the old ladies in the church try to set him up with their granddaughters. The single women are secretly wishing he would ask them out. But he doesn't date—ever. And then out of the blue, he starts seeing someone.

She attends one Sunday morning, and though nobody has ever seen her before, every man in the sanctuary is trying his best not to stare at her. And you know why. She is wearing a rather tight dress. She has that way about her—you know, that sexy thing going on. It's in the way she walks and shifts her eyes and moves her mouth. She's pretty, you have to admit, and she does have a very nice figure. She certainly doesn't have saggy knees or even an ounce of that hard-to-lose belly fat! In fact, you're feeling the urge to shove a dozen donuts down her throat to fatten her up, but you behave.

Beyond anything else, though, you're just plain shocked that the pastor of your church—the bachelor who everyone has been trying to set up with a sweet, piano-playing, Christian young woman—has brought *this* woman to church. Trying to adjust your thinking, you tell yourself that he probably brought her in off the street just to share God's love. Completely harmless!

But then she returns Sunday after Sunday. You think, *Our minister is missionary dating!* And you start to see Facebook pictures of them together. She isn't dressed quite as revealing—okay, trashy—as she was the first time you saw her, but she still has that look about her.

One Sunday morning your pastor stands up at the front of the church and awkwardly proclaims, "Uh…I have an announcement."

He clears his throat, fidgets with his tie, and continues. "Many of you have met my friend Gomer. Well, uh…I believe God has told me to marry her."

You gasp. Everyone around you is visibly shocked. People try to hide their surprise—and disappointment. But no one in that building is more shocked than Gomer.

She sits up a little straighter as the pastor continues, "Uh, Gomer…" He leaves the pulpit and walks to the first row of pews where she is seated, then kneels before her, and says, "I believe you are the woman God has chosen for me. Will you marry me?"

Gomer is absolutely shocked. Is this for real? Does he really love her this much? After all, he knows who she truly is, doesn't he? Her eyes well up with tears, and all she can do is nod yes. He lifts her hand to his lips and kisses it. You are dumbfounded, and as soon as the service has ended, you and your friend rush out to the parking lot to talk. "Can you believe it? Has he lost his mind?" you ask her. "She's not good enough for him! He deserves better. Of all the good, pure, lovely girls he could have chosen, why did he choose her?"

Soon the wedding day arrives. You sit in the same pew you were sitting in when the radical proposal occurred. The music begins. Hosea's not-so-proud mama slinks down the aisle, eyes staring into the ugly green carpet. And then the wedding march begins.

Gomer's parents aren't at the wedding. No surprise there, considering they've been emotionally absent her entire life. So Gomer walks down the aisle alone. You scrutinize her and have to admit she's a pretty bride. After all, isn't every bride beautiful on her wedding day? You notice a slight change in her. She looks a little less confident, a little less sexy, a little softer. Is that a glow you detect? Her eyes dart back and forth as if she is the most surprised woman in the church. Though veiled in lace, she doesn't look completely sure-footed. In fact, she looks a little bit nervous. She is wearing a wedding gown, but she looks more like a girl playing dress-up than a bride. The whole scene is so surreal that you try to dismiss your thoughts and focus on the wedding cake to follow. *Hmmm...I wonder if the frosting will be whipped cream or buttercream?*

Hosea and Gomer both say "I do," and in no time, the wedding is over, rice has been thrown, and the happy couple has headed off on their honeymoon.

"He married *her*?" It's the question everyone at the reception is asking. "Why would he marry *her*?"

And that's the same thing I'm asking centuries later. *Why did he marry her?* Okay, I know the right answer—the Bible answer. Hosea married Gomer, who would be unfaithful to him, as a picture of God's love for the unfaithful nation of Israel. But let's get back to right here, right now. If this happened in my church, I would wonder big time, wouldn't you?

And do you know why I'd wonder? Because deep down, I believe that Gomer is not good enough for Hosea. She is dirty. He is clean. She is full of flaws. He is fabulous. She is not trustworthy. He is too trusting. She is a nobody. He is a somebody.

She does not deserve his attention—or his love.

How would you feel if you were in that church on their wedding day? Would you feel that Gomer deserved to be married to a man like Hosea? Now transfer that to the picture of God and Israel or, closer to home, God and you.

Jesus said, "God never overlooks a single [canary]. And he pays even greater attention to you, down to the last detail—even numbering the hairs on your head!" (Luke 12:6-7 MSG).

God never overlooks you! Why does God love you like that? Why does He accept the imperfect you? After all, compared to His purity, aren't you dirty? So what is God's love for you based on? Why in the world does He choose you, accept you, and love you?

God's Love Is Scandalous

Hosea's love for Gomer surely created a stir around Israel. It was simply scandalous that a prophet would court—and then marry— a woman with her reputation. A situation like this would have made some folks—religious folks, especially—question Hosea's character, wouldn't it?

If Hosea's love for Gomer is a picture of God's love for Israel and for us, what does that say about God? What does that say about us? How did this scandalous love come to be? Did God see Israel— and us—and become filled with pity that turned to love? This passage from the book of Deuteronomy answers that last question:

> For you are a holy people to the LORD your God; the LORD your God has chosen you to be a people for His own possession out of all the peoples who are on the face of the earth. The LORD did not set His love on you nor choose you because you were more in number than any of the peoples, for you were the fewest of all peoples, but because the LORD loved you and kept the oath which He swore to your forefathers, the LORD brought you out by a mighty hand and redeemed you from the house of slavery, from the hand of Pharaoh king of Egypt.
>
> Deuteronomy 7:6-8 NASB

God clearly chose and loved Israel. The love was a "just because" kind of love. It wasn't because they were especially loyal or lovely. God simply chose them and loved them.

God chooses you and loves you too (see John 15:16). It isn't because you are especially loyal or lovely either. He loves you with that same "just because" kind of love He had for Israel.

So when did that love happen? When did God start loving you? After all, you—unlike the nation of Israel—don't have your own private verse in the Bible documenting it! Was it on the day you said "I do" that His love for you began? Or did His love for you start on the same day He made you, created you, and gave you life?

Have you ever thought, *How could a pure, perfect God accept me or even love me? If He places His affection on me, doesn't that diminish Him? Isn't He above loving me?* I have struggled with these very thoughts!

The more I try to see the *me* in Gomer, the more I have to honestly deal with these questions. Over and over, I see this God—this long-suffering, emotional God who loves me no matter what. To me that is scandalous.

So let's just deal with it, okay?

To even begin to grasp the magnitude of God's love toward us, we need to *shift our focus*. We need to focus on Him and His nature—and His nature is love.

God says that He has loved us with an everlasting love (Jeremiah 31:3). When did "everlasting" begin? And when does it end?

God's love never had a starting date. Because He is eternal, self-existent, so is His love. And if He never started to love, He cannot cease to love.

Love like this is hard to grasp, isn't it? I can't seem to wrap my little brain around that big truth, but I have held it in my arms. All moms have. When our first son, Clayton, was born, something fell out of my heart that I didn't know was in there. When I held those eight pounds, twelve ounces of wonder, I loved him. I didn't start to love him—I already loved him. Before I cradled him, I loved him. Before he cried, I loved his voice. Before he could hold my hand, I held him in my heart. My love for Clayton didn't begin when the cord was cut; it was already there. It's just that when he was finally born, I got to give it to him completely. Ten years later the same thing happened when Connor was born—as if it were the first time all over again.

I love my boys because they are a part of me.

God not only loves you because you are a part of Him, He also loves you because He is love. First John 4:8 states it plain and simple: God is love. He gives us His love because He is love. Nothing external provokes Him to love, and nothing external prohibits His love. He is love. His love is an expression of His nature. When God is hurt, He bleeds love because He is love.

> God set His love upon us
> because He is love.

God didn't wring His hands, furrow His brow, and attempt to analyze if you would qualify for His love. In many ways He didn't make a decision to love you or not to love you. His essence is love, so for Him to know you is to love you. For Him to see you is to love you. But God knew we would look in the mirror and see our flawed, imperfect, wandering selves and question if He really could love us. So He proved it:

> This is how God showed his love among us: He sent his one and only Son into the world that we might live through him. This is love: not that we loved God, but that he loved us and sent his Son as an atoning sacrifice for our sins.
>
> 1 John 4:9-10

Jesus is the proof of God's love.

You are loved because God is love. It is that simple, that deep, that profound. That scandalous!

God's love is something you humbly accept by faith, for to reject His love is to reject Him. To say you are not worthy of His love is to say He is not worthy of being love. To say you are not good enough for His love is to say He is not good enough. To deny that God's love applies to you is to reduce the sacrifice of Christ and dismiss part of the character of God. Oh, Gomer girl, I know you don't think about all that when you start feeling unloved or invisible, but perhaps considering those thoughts will help you begin to receive God's love because of who He is, regardless of how you feel.

Watching Gomer walk down the aisle, it's easy to think that she is just not worthy of Hosea's love—duty, maybe, but not love. She was not, is not, and will never be the object of his love. Yet if we reject Gomer's acceptability, we reject our own. If we can't believe that Gomer is loved, we probably won't believe that we too are loved.

If we cop the pose of low spiritual self-esteem, we are not only reducing our own worth, we are also diminishing God. I know you don't *mean* to do that when you take on the "not me, not-good-enough" mindset. Of course not! That's never my intention either. But that's what I was doing during my media mania at the lake. And that's what I'm doing whenever I compare myself to others and find myself stuck in an identity crisis.

I'm making a big deal about God's love because it *is* a big deal. It's the biggest deal ever!

> Because God is love, we are loved.
> We are God's beloved.

Think about this: You are God's beloved. That is your identity.

Can you just say that out loud? And if someone is around, whisper it if you need to: "I am loved because God is love." Good! Now say it again: "I am loved because God is love."

That is true, my fellow Gomer. We are loved because God is love. We are His beloved.

I would like to announce right here, right now, that you actually do have your very own private verse documenting God's love for you. It reminds you that you are God's beloved, and He's crazy about you:

I am my beloved's, and his desire is for me.

Song of Solomon 7:10 NASB

God's desire is for you. His eye is on you. The greatest gift of love you could ever receive is His attention. That's why when you feel invisible, it's so painful. We have such a desire to be seen, to be noticed, to be acknowledged. But, remember, you are never overlooked by God. He loves you, and His desire is for you. You are His beloved.

That's who is reading this book right now—God's chosen and beloved. I am honored!

His Love Makes Us Lovely

Let's pop back to the church where Gomer and Hosea pledged their wedding vows. Months have passed, and you notice Gomer—the new Mrs. Hosea —walk by you in the hallway. She has a radiance about her that she didn't used to have. She seems lovely—no longer sexy, but lovely. *How sweet*, you think as you pass by the table of donuts and coffee and head into the sanctuary.

You sit in church, trying to pay attention to the sermon but unable to think about anything except Gomer. You wonder if she looked that lovely when she was dating Hosea. No, you remember that even on her wedding day, she did not radiate the loveliness she radiated today. She was pretty, but in a clumsy sort of way. But now there's no denying that she is truly lovely. Why is that? And you tear up when it hits you—Hosea's love is what made her lovely.

It is God's love that makes us lovely.

Gomer isn't the woman she once was. She has been made new. She is pure. You realize that you no longer think of her as "that woman"—the one you wanted to force-feed donuts to and shield your husband's eyes from. You no longer think of her as trashy. Instead, she's beautiful...new...lovely.

It was his love—his love made her lovely.

Just like Gomer, you are loved. God chose you. He loved you while you were still dirty. The Bible says He loved you while you were still a sinner (see Romans 5:8). God didn't choose to love you because you were already lovely; He loved you and *then* you became lovely. Your value comes from His inherent value.

Just like Hosea chose to love Gomer, and God chose to love Israel, God chooses to love you—the real you, the imperfect you. Look into the mirror of your soul and see Gomer reflected back at you. She was the beloved bride, and so are you. You're already loved, so you just need to embrace how God sees you. Yet how do you do this—especially on those days when you feel like you don't measure up?

Let's begin by acknowledging something very important: You are not your current failures or your past mistakes. You are not your successes or your virtues. You are not what you do, what you did, what you haven't done, what you should have done, or what you wish you'd done. You are not what you have gone through. You are not what someone else has said about you. You are not a nobody! You are a chosen, loved woman whom God calls His beloved.

His beloved—that is who God sees when He looks at you. Can you begin to accept the you who God sees?

Here's an assignment for you—one that will help you start seeing yourself as God sees you. Grab a pen and write down the following statements on Post-it notes and stick them everywhere! Or go buy some cheap lipstick from the Dollar Store and use it to write these truths on your bathroom mirror or your windshield. Come on! I dare you! Read them over and over and recite them to yourself so you can start identifying with the *you* God sees:

- God loves me, and His love makes me lovely.
- I am loved because God is love.
- I am not the be-tolerated; I am the beloved!

Yes! You are God's beloved, and so am I. Let's both try to trust God more with our feelings when it comes to this, okay? You may not feel loved or accepted, but how you feel does not define who you are. You may feel invisible, but you are not. You are seen and loved and appreciated.

So when you start to feel like a nobody—unlovable, rejected, unaccepted, or invisible—remember that your opinion is not the final word on this matter. Trust God's opinion on this one, sister! Say those three truths out loud over and over. Say them so often that if anyone says to you, "Tell me who you are?" you'll completely forget to mention your name as you shout out, "I am loved because God is love!" and "I am not the be-tolerated; I am the beloved!" and "God's love makes me lovely!"

You won't see yourself as the woman who cleaned tables in the Baylor cafeteria saw herself—a nobody, someone not worth getting to know. You'll see yourself as a somebody—God's lovely somebody.

Nice to meet you, you lovely thing!

3

When You Say "I Do" to I AM

"In the very place where they were once named Nobody, they will be named God's Somebody."

HOSEA 1:10 MSG

Fall means speaking engagement season for me, and with that comes the task of choosing what to wear for my various appearances. Now, because I travel to different places, I can wear the same outfits again and again! As I set about choosing this autumn's attire, I pulled some favorite jeans—a pair I'd worn the previous year—off of a hanger. As I tried on—or tried to try on—the jeans, I realized that something had happened. They were a little snug, actually a lot snug! I couldn't pull them up. Either the jeans had shrunk or I had grown. So I stepped on my talking scale to hear if I'd gained weight, but it only registered one pound higher than I'd been the last time I'd weighed myself. Was my scale wrong?

You might not think of a scale as your best friend, but mine is interesting because it talks. It uses the most dignified British accent to announce my weight. I suppose its manufacturer thought the number would be less offensive if it were spoken so politely! Sometimes I wish it would say, "So sorry to tell you, ma'am, your weight is ____. However, you certainly are cute!" In fact, when my husband steps on my talking scale, it says, "One at a time please!" (Kidding!)

All that to say my scale really is reliable. So I called a friend—someone my own age—and whined, "My weight has barely changed, but my jeans don't fit me anymore!"

"Go to Dillard's and find the intimates department and ask for a woman named Julia," my friend promptly advised. "She will help you. She can make your clothes fit."

Off to Dillard's I went. I found the intimates department, located Julia, and whispered to her, "My clothes don't fit. Body parts have moved."

Julia assured me that she had just the thing to fix my problem and asked me to wait while she went and got it. She returned with a little package and a promising solution: "You wear this under your clothes. It stretches from the top of your knees to the top of your ribs. It will smooth everything in between."

She then placed the tiniest piece of shriveled fabric in my hands. It was the size of an infant Ace Bandage that had been in the dryer for about 12 years. It reminded me of the pantyhose I used to see hanging from my grandmother's shower curtain rod—all shriveled, puckered, and shrunken.

As I fingered this teeny scrap of fabric, I thought, *There's no way a woman can put this on her body and live to tell about it!*

Nevertheless, I walked into the fitting room, took a deep

breath—which could have been my last breath—and tugged and pulled that minuscule piece of spandex onto my body.

"Wow!" is all I could say once I'd wrestled it on. I could breathe. I was smoothed out. My rolls were flattened. My bumps were gone. Now, the disclaimer is that I had really pudgy knees and a triple chin because, of course, that fat has to go somewhere, but I was sold! I told Julia to please ring me up because I was ready to become the proud owner of my very first set of Spanx.

Spanx have changed my life while allowing my wardrobe to remain the same! In fact, I love them so much that I wrote a little verse about them:

> If any woman be in Spanx, she is a new creation.
> Old rolls are tucked away; Behold,
> All things have become smooth!

Okay, you probably recognized that unique rendition of 2 Corinthians 5:17. Here's the real verse: "If any man be in Christ, he is a new creature: old things are passed away; behold, all things are become new" (KJV).

Being clothed in Spanx didn't change the true me; it *hid* the true me. But when we are in Christ—when we are clothed in His righteousness—we are made new. You are a new you, and the new you is the *true* you.

When you say "I do" to Jesus, you are the beloved, which is your new identity in Christ.

When Gomer said "I do" to Hosea, she was no longer Gomer the prostitute. She became Gomer the beloved bride, the chosen wife.

> When we say "I do" to I AM, we become the beloved.

Since our new identity in Christ is our true identity, we want to live like it, don't we?

So how do you live like it? How do you leave the past behind you, or as my friend Lori says, "leave your behind in the past"?

Forget the Former Things

Some of us said "I do" to Jesus just like Gomer said "I do" to Hosea, but we live the "I'm not." In other words, we receive forgiveness and new life in Christ, but then we quickly go back to living old patterns and believing old lies: *I'm not good enough. I'm not worthy of His love. He couldn't really love someone like me.*

Because God chose you and loved you, that frees you to live as the true *you.* You don't need to dwell upon your past any longer. In fact, in order to not dwell *in* your past, you can't dwell *on* your past. That was then; this is now! Isaiah 43:18-19 says, "Forget the former things; do not dwell on the past. See, I am doing a new thing! Now it springs up; do you not perceive it?"

Oh, girl, I want—need—to dwell in the present truth of who I am in Christ, and I know you want to dwell there too. Our feelings are so powerful, and they can shout so loudly: *You aren't really loved—you are just tolerated! You will only be accepted by God if your behavior is acceptable to Him!* And those feelings can yank us right out of the present truth of our identity in Christ and straight into an identity crisis. So let me give you, my fellow Gomer, three key truths—powerful statements backed up by powerful Scripture— you can tell yourself over and over to help you dwell in present truth.

Three Key Truths
Truth #1

Are you ready for your first truth? Here it is: *I am dearly loved.* Colossians 3:12 says, "Therefore, as God's chosen people, holy and dearly loved, clothe yourselves with compassion, kindness, humility, gentleness and patience."

Gomer was dearly loved. Israel was dearly loved. You are dearly loved. This is the reality you dwell in—the reality you need to tell yourself.

A study published in the *Journal of Personality and Social Psychology* * shows that addressing yourself in the second person "you" or in the third person—using your own name—is the most effective way to speak to yourself. In the study some participants were instructed to talk to themselves in the first person—for example, saying, "I am capable"—before they did something stressful, while others were told to use second-person pronouns ("You are capable") or their own names ("Jennifer is capable").

The people who used "you" and their own names felt more positive about themselves *and* performed better. The study also found that they felt less shame and self-doubt. The lesson here? I should

---

* Ethan Kross, et al., "Self-Talk as a Regulatory Mechanism: How You Do It Matters," *Journal of Personality and Social Psychology* 106, no. 2 (2014): 304-24.

say, "Jennifer is loved" or "You are loved" rather than "I am loved." Changing a few little words can make a big difference!

Now, I share this with you because I happen to know that you talk to yourself. We all do! And since you do, I want you to tell yourself the truth in the best possible way—the way that will get through to you and give you reassurance that you're a somebody who matters. So say it with me right now: "[Your name] is loved!"

Truth #2

Powerful truth number two is this: *I am accepted.* God backs up this truth in His Word: "to the praise of the glory of His grace, by which He made us accepted in the Beloved" (Ephesians 1:6 NKJV).

Gomer was accepted by Hosea. Israel was accepted by God. And you are also accepted by God. That is the reality in which you dwell. Amazing, isn't it? You are not only accepted in the beloved, you are accepted *by* the beloved Himself—God. You have value. You have worth. You are visible to Him!

When you accepted Christ, He accepted you. You may sometimes feel rejected, but how you feel is not who you are! You are accepted, acceptable—no exception! So find a mirror right now, look into it, and repeat the following words: "You are accepted."

Truth #3

Here's the final truth to tell yourself: *I am complete.* Colossians 2:10 says, "You are complete in Him, who is the head of all principality and power" (NKJV).

When you said "I do" to Christ, you became complete in Him. He gives you Himself completely. We are complete when we are found in Him. When we have Christ, we have no need for anything more. Now, Gomer girl, we can still sometimes feel unfulfilled, but discontentment is a feeling, not a reality you dwell in!

When you said "I do," when you became a Christian, you were instantly—*poof!*—made spiritually whole.

When Jesus died on the cross, His final words were, "It is finished." And when He said it, He meant it—it is finished, completed. So it's time to look in the mirror and say that truth to yourself: "[Your name], you are complete!"

> You are loved. You are accepted. You are complete.

L-A-C

Now, Gomer girl, please notice something. When you speak these truths to yourself in the order I gave them to you, you say, "I am *loved*. I am *accepted*. I am *complete*." Look at the first letters of those three words: L-A-C. They make a word—a misspelled word, but still a word—that you can remember: *lac*. It may be spelled wrong, but the message is right. You and I *lack* nothing in Christ. In Him we are new creations—loved, accepted, and complete.

The mirror of God's Word reflects the truth of who you are—the visible, lovely *you* who is God's beloved. Did you know that the Bible is compared to a mirror? The mirrors in your home and at the stores are flawed, making your image ever-so-slightly distorted. The Bible, though, is perfect. It's the only mirror you can look into and actually see the truth.

If you looked into your bathroom mirror this morning and saw a streak of toothpaste smeared across your cheek, you wouldn't leave the bathroom before wiping it off, would you? You wouldn't walk away from the mirror and immediately forget what you looked like just because you weren't staring at your reflection, would you? Of course not!

We do, however, tend to forget what we see in the mirror of Scripture, which can affect our identity and our sense of security. James 1:23-24 says, "Anyone who listens to the word but does not do what it says is like someone who looks at his face in a mirror and, after looking at himself, goes away and immediately forgets what he looks like."

What James is pointing out here is that when we hear something but have no response to it, we're like someone who glances in the mirror but then forgets what she looks like. I've always thought of that passage as only referring to our sin that is revealed in the mirror. But I've come to understand that James is also referring to all truth, which includes the truth that we are loved, accepted, and complete.

Isn't that encouraging to know? If you look into the mirror of God's Word, you'll see truth! And you'll see what you look like in God's eyes—a beloved, accepted, and complete woman of God.

One teeny, weeny caution, though. The point of looking in the mirror is not to find yourself and discover your own importance. The point of looking in the mirror is to find God and to understand that you are found in Him. Looking into the mirror of God's Word gives you a true view of God, which grants you a right view of yourself. A right assessment of yourself includes both your prone-to-wander tendencies *and* your incredible value.

> God reveals the truth about us so we can reflect the truth about Him.

Even if mirrors make you nervous—even if you're worried you'll see saggy knees or a triple chin—be sure to look into the mirror of truth every day to see who you really are. And then get out there and live what you learn. Practice what you perceive.

Let's not just hear—let's *do*. Let's say "I Do" to I AM every time we gaze into the mirror of God's Word.

I do believe the truth that I am loved.

I do agree with the truth that I am accepted.

I do trust the truth that I am complete in Christ.

Isn't your identity in Christ beautiful? You're spiritually whole... lovely...valuable. Even though my eyes are blind, I like what I see when I look into the mirror of truth. Don't you?

God loves me
and
His love
makes me
lovely.

#TheInvisibleBook

4

Married with Children

*So he went and took Gomer the
daughter of Diblaim, and she
conceived and bore him a son.*

HOSEA 1:3 NKJV

If I were to tweet out Gomer and Hosea's strange love story or reduce it to a series of Facebook posts, this is how it would read:

Spiritual guy pursues scandalous girl (#unbelievable).

Sincere guy dates skeptical girl (#ishecrazy).

God-centered guy marries self-centered girl (#luckygirl).

Devalued daughter becomes highly valued bride (#beautiful).

Aimless woman becomes chosen wife (#amazinggrace).

What a love story! In spite of the odds, our girl, Gomer, is invisible no more. She said "I do" and became the chosen, loved Mrs. Hosea!

So the guy has proposed, the wedding has taken place, and the beautiful bride has been whisked away on her honeymoon. But now the honeymoon is over, and Gomer has settled into life as a married woman. Men still turn their heads when she walks into a room, but Gomer is different now. Not only is she strikingly beautiful, but she also glows. She glows like a woman who is loved and is in love.

What a life! Gomer has never felt so secure. She adores her new little house. She delights in cooking dinner every night. She dreams up ways to surprise Hosea on Saturdays and arranges outings for them. She chooses cute nighties for bedtime, always applies a little lip gloss before Hosea gets home from work, and makes sure she hugs him as soon as he walks in the door. Yes, she's living a life of married bliss.

When you see Gomer at church on Sundays, you notice she's chatty and smiling. She's become one of the girls. Women flock to her, desiring her friendship. She has a way about her that makes you want to hang out with her. You continue to marvel at the change you've seen in her. What a transformation! And you can tell that Hosea is very happy too.

Gomer's life is dreamy. Her marriage seems like a fairy tale. In fact, the story is far more amazing than anyone could have ever imagined.

As the months pass, though, Gomer finds herself not as eager to make dinner or as excited to apply lip gloss. She doesn't come to church as often. You overhear Hosea being asked, "Where's your wife?" You see him awkwardly glance down and mutter, "Uh...at home. She isn't feeling so well."

It's true. Gomer *doesn't* feel well. In fact, it's all she can do to get off the couch. She's exhausted. She's lost her dazzle, her spark, her interest in Hosea—and her interest in everything else. She cries over the smallest things. Her feelings are hurt if Hosea says the wrong thing—or if he says the right thing at the wrong time or in the wrong way. What is happening to her? Is the fairy tale fading?

Actually the fairy tale isn't fading. It's merely changing—along with the rest of her body. You may have guessed it. Gomer is pregnant! She and Hosea are about to become parents. As her belly swells, her glow returns. She's excited to become a mom. And she's determined that she will be a better mother to her child than her own mother was to her. Better yet, she is so thankful to have a man like Hosea as the father of her child. After all, his name means "salvation."

Gomer knows better than anyone else that the meaning of Hosea's name fits him perfectly. Hosea saved *her*—saved her from her past, saved her from her insecurity, and saved her from her fear of the future. He has been her salvation. And while Hosea is a bit nervous about becoming a dad, he starts spending his Saturdays building a crib. Life is beautiful, and Gomer and Hosea couldn't be happier.

Then one day the baby is born. It's a boy! His name is Jezreel—which means "God scatters" (Hosea 1:4).

As the marriage of Hosea and Gomer represented God's relationship with Israel, the names of their children were also part of God's message to His people. God told Hosea to name their firstborn Jezreel to show that He was going to put an end to the leadership of the house of Israel. I wonder what happy Gomer thought of that? It was an ominous prediction caught up in the name of her firstborn. Perhaps she was too busy changing diapers, nursing, and gazing into that baby's beautiful brown eyes to spend much time pondering the prophecy.

Not many months passed before Jezreel was off and crawling, making messes, and getting into everything. Soon he could use a sippy cup and was well on his way to becoming a big boy. In the midst of all this, it happened again—that same tiredness over-whelmed Gomer. But this time she was a little wiser to the situation and headed straight to the local market to purchase a pregnancy test. Sure enough, the results in the window registered as positive.

Nine months later, Gomer gave birth to a baby girl.

This time God told Hosea to name the baby Lo-Ruhamah (Hosea 1:6), which meant "not pitied." Now, the proud daddy was also a keen prophet, so he realized right away what God was telling the nation of Israel through the name of his baby girl. God would no longer have compassion on the house of Israel.

Former swinging single Gomer was now home all day with a baby and a toddler—and she was exhausted. As she changed dia-pers and swayed in the rocking chair, she found herself daydream-ing about how exciting her life used to be—before Hosea and the kids. Trying to shake those memories from her mind, Gomer forced herself to focus on her wedding day, her honeymoon, her man…until it happened again!

Hosea and Gomer's third child was born—another boy. Once again God supplied the baby's name, which was Lo-Ammi or "not my people" (Hosea 1:9). Hosea and Gomer's youngest son's name meant that eventually God's tolerance would run out, and He would no longer call Israel His own.

Wandering Ways

Tough stuff, isn't it? Back in the day, though, it wasn't uncommon for God to communicate His message through names. Remember what Hosea meant? Salvation. And Gomer's father's name? Well, never mind that one! God was using the names of Hosea and Gomer's children to try to get Israel to wake up and pay attention. He had chosen the people of Israel as His own, but they weren't living like God's beloved. Prone to wander, they were straying from Him in a major way. And God was letting them know that if they persisted in their wandering ways, they would put Him in the dreadful position of having to abandon them.

Gomer was a mother and Hosea was a father. They were human—just like you and me. They loved their children, and God loved their children too. The children's names didn't mean that God had forsaken those little ones or loved them any less. The meanings of their names were simply part of the word picture God was communicating through Hosea, the prophet, and his family to the nation of Israel.

Now with three young children to care for, Gomer's life had completely changed. These days dinner was rarely ready when Hosea arrived home. And forget about dressing up—Gomer's regular uniform nowadays was a food-stained, frumpy old T-shirt and a pair of mom jeans. Lip gloss? She couldn't even find a tube—even if she'd had the time to apply it! Forever picking up toys, she had zero energy for picking out attractive nighties. At the end of the day, she was grateful to grab one of Hosea's undershirts, throw it on, and fall exhausted into bed.

It wasn't that Gomer no longer desired Hosea. She was just starting to desire other things also. You know, something more exciting, something easier, something more freeing—something to make her feel like *somebody* because she was right back to feeling like an overlooked, unimportant, invisible nobody.

Can you relate to Gomer at all? Do you know what it's like to feel swallowed up in the dailiness of your life—doing the same old chores over and over and over again? Do you ever feel stuck in something that should feel special? Do you ever feel invisible in the midst of your circumstances?

I do. I think we all do from time to time.

When I was a young mom, I remember one particular night when Clayton was 13 years old and about as emotionally exhausting as a child could be. "Why can't I..." or "How come everyone else is allowed to..." and "That isn't fair!" were the phrases I was constantly combatting all day long. And I mean A-L-L day long! At the same time, I had three-year-old Connor, who was physically exhausting—busy, active, and loud! One of his favorite things to do was pull all the pots and pans from the cabinet and bang on them with wooden spoons. So while Clayton was draining my brain, Connor was wearing me out!

One night, to escape the constant interrogation from budding lawyer Clayton and the banging and clanging of little drummer Connor, I escaped into my closet and shut the door. I tried to ease my tension by doing some Lamaze breathing—you think that is only for the pain of childbirth? Sister, you need that for the pain of child rearing! After a few deep breaths, I thought I could face them again without screaming or crying. I don't mean their screaming or crying—I mean mine! What I really wanted to do was run away from home!

When the drumming ended, I heard Connor asking Clayton, "Where's Mommy?"

"I dunno," Clayton grunted.

Evidently, though, they discussed this enough to send out a search party. I heard them calling, but I didn't answer. I heard them opening and closing doors, but I stayed hidden behind mine.

"Maybe she's in the backyard," Clayton said. They went outside but were back inside in no time. I soon heard them coming down the hall, knocking on my bedroom door, calling, "*Mom! Mommy!*"

I must admit I will win no Mom-of-the-Year awards for what I'm about to tell you. I ignored them. I so wanted to disappear that I didn't answer them. I thought, *I've had it. They'll be fine. Clay can take care of Connor for just a little while. Heck, he can raise him. He clearly has this parenting thing down!*

Then I heard Connor ask, "Can I have a Capri Sun?"

"Sure! Go get one," Clayton replied.

Well, that's all it took. There was no way my three-year-old was going to open one of those exploding juice grenades all by himself! I bolted out of the closet and into the kitchen.

Now, wouldn't you think that someone at that point would have asked, "Where were you?" Nope! Connor just asked for some cookies, and Clayton launched into a closing argument about why he was innocent of the juice that was splattered all over the kitchen!

I know I'm not alone here. Every mom has had those moments when she gets familiarity fatigue and just wants to hide or escape, right?

You would think the familiar would be a reassuring place, but sometimes we can feel stuck in the familiar. And those feelings can be dangerous. We find ourselves searching for a door of escape, but it often leads us from our First Love into the wilderness of self.

It just doesn't seem right that something as amazing as motherhood or as beautiful as Gomer's new life could ever get old. Something as astounding as our own chosenness should never tarnish, should it? But it does.

> Nothing should cease to be to us wonderful, or sublime, because it is familiar. The rising of the sun should be as great a miracle to us, as the rising of a human being from the dead. Strictly considered, one is as great a miracle as the other. They both illustrate the character and attributes of God, and his unceasing agency is in every phenomenon which takes place in the world. But there is evidently this tendency of the mind to overlook the beautiful, the wonderful, the great, when they have once become familiar things.
>
> Christopher P. Cranch, *The Western Messenger*

When something becomes familiar, it can be overlooked. Let me ask you this: *What truth about you is so familiar that you are prone to overlook it?* Carefully consider this question. Ask God to reveal the answer to you. Your answer matters because *you* matter.

Contempt or Contentment

Do you find yourself overlooking how much God loves you because you're so used to hearing about His love at church or reading about it in the Bible? You've heard the old Aesop saying

"Familiarity breeds contempt," haven't you? Well, contempt is the feeling that a person or thing is worthless or beneath consideration. When something—like your incredible value and God's scandalous love for you—becomes familiar to you, you risk disregarding it, devaluing it, or overlooking it.

Familiarity does not need to breed contempt, though. Familiarity can instead bring contentment. It all depends on what we see in the familiar.

> When we overlook truth, we will
> only see what we lack.

Gomer must have overlooked what she had and, instead, focused on what she lacked. She now had three little kids and a husband who was often away preaching. She used to have to swat the men away, and now all she was doing was swatting little toddler bottoms and flies out of her kitchen.

Think about it. Before she became Mrs. Hosea, she was Go-Go-Gomer! She was out every night. Not only that, but she was with a different man every night. Men flirted with her, bought her dinner, and showered her with attention. When Gomer was first married, she didn't miss the hordes of men. She treasured feeling loved and being Hosea's one and only. But then the honeymoon ended.

Freshness always fades into familiarity. Even when we can't

imagine it happening, it always does. Hosea became more and more familiar the longer he and Gomer were married. Things just didn't feel the same as they first did. The miracle that Hosea had chosen her had lost its luster.

When the kids first came along, Gomer was into it. She was determined to be the best mom ever! But three kids later...Well, same ol', same ol'. Instead of focusing on what was right with her life, she started to focus on what was wrong. It was as if she'd just blended into the busy background of her life—unseen and overlooked by Hosea and the children. She couldn't shake the feeling that she was only as valuable as what she did for everyone around her—making dinner, changing diapers, cleaning house, bringing casseroles to church, taking Hosea's suits to the cleaners. Her time was filled with family duties, but her mind was beginning to wander. Who *was* she, anyway?

Gomer may have still been physically present at home doing the wife/mom thing, but her mind was elsewhere. Her hands may have been busy at home, but her heart was headed out. She may have been living in the reality that she was loved and chosen, but she was starting to neglect that truth, and her discontent was growing.

Familiarity did not bring contentment to Gomer. Instead, familiarity bred contempt.

It wasn't that something was really wrong; it just didn't feel right. Was this really the life she'd signed up for? It had been exciting and fulfilling—at first. Hosea was her first love—her only real love—and at the beginning that had been enough. But now something inside Gomer was stirring.

> When we're stuck in the rut of sameness, we fail to notice that we already have everything we need.

She was starting to feel familiarity fatigue! And, sister, don't we all? Even when the familiar stuff is good stuff, it's easy to get tired. Life can become so routine that we fail to see its beauty. We can get stuck in the rut of sameness and forget to notice that we have everything we need. Instead, we wonder about what we lack, and it leads to wandering.

Gomer began to wander. And her wandering didn't start the moment she walked out her front door. It began the way wandering always begins—in her head.

Wandering Thoughts

Just like Gomer, we live out our new and true identity in the dailiness of life. We—the chosen, beloved of God—are surrounded by dirty diapers, ungrateful bosses, endless deadlines, media messages, pressure to perform, messy homes, unpaid bills...And the list goes on. Though the God of eternity calls us His own, we live out our identity here on this planet and in our humanity. And it ain't always pretty, is it?

Often the dailiness of *where* we are distracts us from the dignity of *who* we are. And sometimes, like Gomer, we can become so familiar with the astounding truth of our own chosenness that the miraculous truth loses its luster. That's when we begin to feel invisible, as if we no longer matter to anyone. And then the questions of self-doubt begin: *Am I good enough? Who am I, anyway? Does anyone even notice me? Is this really all there is? I wonder what it would be like if...*

Now, it's easy to become restless when we're stuck in a routine day after day. It makes sense that we might start to feel unmoored by the very things that once made us feel secure. When we start to question why we are doing the same things over and over again, it's tempting to let our minds follow a new, unknown path. And as we focus on who we are and what we do in this world, it's easy to become overly self-aware and eventually self-absorbed. *I need to do more with my life than this,* we think. *Why does everyone else seem to have more friends than I do?,* we wonder. *I need more to make myself happy,* we surmise. We're no longer stuck in a rut. We're stuck in insecurity.

The more our minds wander, the more we seek to alleviate our confusion and get our sense of identity back—even though we never lost it.

Our situations haven't changed, but our thinking has.

Corrupt vs. Correct Thinking

Without even realizing it, mired in discontent we trade in correct thinking for corrupt thinking when we wander from God. Correct thinking says, *I am the beloved. God loves me, and His love makes me lovely. God sees me and knows who I am.* Corrupt thinking replies, *Well, I don't feel like the beloved. God doesn't love me completely; after all, I'm not really lovely or lovable. I feel invisible. It's time for me to go find myself.*

Oh, Gomer girl, we've got to trust that God loves us because

He is love. When we neglect the truth of who God is, we eventually reject the truth of who we are.

Yes, there will be days when you feel unworthy, unseen, unacceptable—oh, just let me say it—like a saggy-kneed loser! (At least I have those days!) We all have those days when we neglect the truth of our chosenness. We focus less on who we are in Christ and more on how we feel about ourselves. And the longer we neglect the truth, the sooner we'll just flat out reject the truth.

> When we begin to neglect—and then reject—truth, we trade in correct thinking for corrupt thinking.

That is what Gomer did, and that is what humans have done since the beginning of time. Just pop over to the base of Mount Sinai with me for a few paragraphs, and you'll see what I mean. This story is found in Exodus 32, if you want to look it up later. But for now I'll summarize.

Picture a band of weary wilderness wanderers with their leader away on a mountain for more than a month. God had delivered the Israelites out of slavery in Egypt, and they were on their way to their own land—the Promised Land. But they needed to stop at Sinai because their leader, Moses, had an appointment with God.

And what a long appointment it was! Moses had been up on that mountain listening to God for forty days. In the meantime the wanderers were becoming restless. They had grown weary of resting in the comfort of being the chosen, beloved people of God. Instead of keeping their minds on the God who had rescued them from slavery, they focused their eyes on the sorry trappings of their temporary rest stop. The familiarity of their chosenness had not brought them contentment—it had bred contempt. They had lost focus of what was correct, and they became corrupted. That's how Exodus 32:7 describes it: "Then the LORD said to Moses, 'Go down, because your people, whom you brought up out of Egypt, have become corrupt.'"

It's no surprise what happened next. The Israelites' corrupt thinking led to corrupt actions. Instead of staying faithful to the one true God who had brought them out of Egypt, they decided they wanted a new god. So they asked Moses' brother, Aaron, to make them one. This might sound crazy, but truthfully it's what we all do when we lose our focus on the true God. We make new gods to take His place.

Long before Aaron's hand scooped up the gold needed to make a new god, some incorrect—and corrupt—thinking took place. Corrupt thoughts always precede corrupt actions.

Truth and Temptation

While stay-at-home mom Gomer drooped on her couch daydreaming about how pretty her clothes once were, how handsome men once flirted with her, and how much she adored that buzz, her thoughts were wandering from the truth of who she was to the temptation of who she wanted to be.

We do that too, don't we? We ignore the truth of who we are and give in to the temptation to be something else. We overlook the liberty of our completeness in Christ and accept the lie that we are not enough. Because we are prone to wander, we—like Gomer— find it easy to slip into corrupt thinking, slowly but surely trading the truth for deception.

We all have the restless tendencies of Gomer stuck at home and the antsy Israelites trapped at the base of Mount Sinai. We can get all too familiar with our chosenness. We can treat the truth of our identity with disregard and find ourselves hiding in a closet of confusion.

When I was stalking Facebook that August day at the lake, I was wondering how I could "become as popular as she was" or "feel better about who I was" or "be noticed by more people." I was trading in correct thinking about who I was in Christ for corrupt thinking about who I wasn't according to this world and what I lacked by society's standards.

The more our minds wonder, the more our minds wander!

Oh, sister, beware of *neglecting* the truth of who you are because it will lead you to *rejecting* the truth of who you are.

You are too valuable to God to allow corrupt thinking to confuse you about your identity. How you think will eventually impact what you do. Your thoughts lead to your actions. So before we follow Gomer into the next scene of her story, let's pause and think about our own stories. And let's ask ourselves some important questions:

- How can we prevent corrupt thinking from happening to us?

- How can we experience fresh truth in the familiar?

- How can we stay astounded by our chosenness so that we don't stray from our First Love and our true identity?

- How can we trust that God sees us even when we feel invisible?

Phroneo

One word: *Phroneo*. Okay, okay! One *Greek* word!

When you *phroneo* (yes, it's a verb), you "set your affection on things above, not on things on the earth" (Colossians 3:2 KJV). *Phroneo* means "to set your affection." You *set* it, like cement drying, slowly hardening, becoming *set*.

Slowly but surely you shift your heart's focus from the daily to the Divine, from the world to the Word. Now, I'm not saying you need to sell all of your earthly goods—except that long denim jumper from the '80s—and move to a tent on a mountain far above our modern lives. Nor am I talking about acting so heavenly minded that you become an earthly irritant! We don't need to ignore or dismiss the daily. We just need to make sure we don't fixate on it. While we experience life here below, we also exist on life there above. We must set our affection on God's truth because if we gravitate toward truth, we will navigate toward contentment. But if we gravitate toward seeing all that is wrong with our lives, we will navigate away from seeing all that is right about our lives.

As Proverbs 4:23 says, "Above all else, guard your heart, for everything you do flows from it." We Gomer girls must set our affection on truth so we don't wander off into the tangle of lies. We need to *phroneo* on the One who chose us—God Himself, our First Love—so we don't end up feeling like second choice.

> Where we set our affection is
> where we find our satisfaction.

When we begin to *phroneo* on things above, our hearts seek after higher desires and truer thoughts. When we *phroneo* on things above, our familiar becomes fresh—a window through which we see glimpses of heaven. When we *phroneo* on things above, it becomes harder and harder to entertain corrupt thinking. All of this makes sense because when we *phroneo*, we write truth on a drying slab of concrete.

Now, changing your thinking doesn't happen right away. It's a process—a daily process. It takes time to set our affection on things above just like it takes time for concrete to set. But once concrete is set, it takes an earthquake or a jackhammer to change it, doesn't it? In the same way, our hearts cannot be easily altered once they have been set.

Where we set our affection is where we find our satisfaction. Where we set our affection is where we find our identity. Girl, we gotta *phroneo* on things above!

If we *phroneo* on things above, we set our minds on truth and refuse to settle for lies. Yet if we *phroneo* on things below—if we *phroneo* on our past, our imperfections, our insecurities—we will think corrupt thoughts. If we *phroneo* on things below like Gomer did, we'll miss the astounding in the familiar, the miraculous in

the everyday. And if we *phroneo* on things below—like the Israelites did—we'll keep our eyes focused on the sorry trappings of
this earthly rest stop and believe the lie that God has forgotten us.

So the next time you start to feel a twinge of incorrect thinking, imagine that your mind is always in the process of setting like
slowly drying cement. Don't get set on a lie. Immediately shift that
corrupt thinking back to correct thinking. This will help you to
continually *phroneo*—set your affection—on things above.

When we *phroneo* on God, we have peace. Isaiah 26:3 tells us,
"You keep him in perfect peace whose mind is [set] on you, because
he trusts in you" (ESV).

Gomer girl, let's start the process of setting our mind and our
affection on things above so we won't wonder who we are—and so
we won't begin to wander away from the truth of His love for us.

The Affair

For their mother has played the harlot; She
who conceived them has acted shamefully.
For she said, "I will go after my lovers..."
HOSEA 2:5 NASB

Although Hosea's main preaching gig was in the capital city of
Samaria, he often had to leave town to preach. One evening Gomer
decided that she's going out too—just this once. She asked a neighbor to watch the kids, and then she went back to the old streets she
used to walk—just for a visit. She talked to only one man—just
one little harmless flirtation over dinner. She then hurried home
to tuck her children into bed.

But just this once led to a second time and a third and...as
the allure of her old life became more irresistible, Gomer became
less responsible. Even when Hosea was home, she'd make excuses
about needing to run an errand. She loved the buzz of being free
and feeling desired by other men. It had been so long since she'd

been with another man that she'd forgotten how powerful and independent her flirtations made her feel.

Somewhere in her mind, Gomer had made the shift. She didn't *phroneo* truth, and she stopped seeing herself as Hosea's beloved bride. Unable to see her true self anymore, she started seeing her distorted reflection in the look of a lustful man. It wasn't right, but, she reasoned, at least she felt like *somebody* again.

> When we overlook truth, we
> can't see our own value.

Many nights, I imagine, Hosea would come home at the end of a long day only to find no dinner simmering on the stove and the house a complete wreck. The baby was running around with a diaper that should have been changed hours ago, dirty dishes were cluttering up the counter, and Gomer was just sitting listlessly on the back porch—distant, discontent, and daydreaming. What was going on?

Hosea did his best to reach his distracted wife. He brought home bouquets of her favorite flowers. He tidied the house. He cooked dinner, changed diapers, and tried to get Gomer to talk. But she remained indifferent. Was he losing her?

He began hearing rumors that Gomer had been spotted out with other men. He confronted her, but she denied it. This went on for weeks. Then one day Hosea returned home from work and found a note on the kitchen table. Gomer had written, "The kids are at the neighbors' house. I do love you, but it's just not enough...I will go after my lovers."

So Gomer had done what Hosea knew she would do all along. She had left her identity as a beloved bride and returned to her sketchy past. *What was the reason?* Hosea wondered.

Losing sight of her true self, Gomer had mistakenly thought that other lovers could give her something more than what Hosea had given her. She believed that they would allow her to feel that special something she wasn't feeling while stuck at home with Hosea and the kids. Gomer left Hosea for other lovers because she thought they would give her "my bread and my water, my wool and my flax, my oil and my drink" (Hosea 2:5b NASB).

Yeah, I know. A grocery list is an odd reason to walk away from your marriage, your kids, and your true identity. But the book of Hosea is not only a narrative—it's poetry too. So what do you think Gomer's grocery list actually represented? What was the allure of bread and water, wool and flax, oil and drink? And how would these things cause a woman to turn away from the truth and head in a dangerous direction?

The Danger of Desire

Bread and water are the basics of life—your daily needs being met. Gomer needed bread and water to survive, thrive, and feel secure. Sure, she had a roof over her head and food on the table. Hosea was a good provider. But maybe she longed for something more—fancier furniture to replace that kid-stained sofa, an in-ground pool instead of a backyard sprinkler, and candlelit, five-star restaurant dinners in place of home-cooked meals. Have you felt the same way? You know you should be grateful for what you have, but when you pull up Pinterest or page through a home-decorating magazine, something feels lacking, so your mind begins to wander.

In Gomer's time wool and flax were what women used to make linen. You know, clothes! So wool and flax represented Gomer's wardrobe, her appearance, and the physical impression she made on others. Once again we know that Hosea was a good provider. His wife wasn't lacking in skirts, sandals, and dresses (or yoga pants, Nikes, and North Face jackets), but maybe Gomer wanted a little bit more—something slightly more sparkly, garments of higher-quality fabric, a few more brand-name pieces to set her apart. She wanted to be noticed—and then noticed some more.

And what about oil and drink? I believe these were included on the list because of the pleasure they brought. The sweetness of the grape brought a delight to the soul and a treat to the taste buds. Think about the things that are your go-to for pleasure—your favorite dessert, a refreshing drink, a delicate perfume. What little luxuries make you feel special, cared for, important? Knowing what we know about Gomer's past, we can see where this desire may have carried her.

Now, think about all of these items on Gomer's "grocery list." Is there anything wrong with bread and water, wool and flax, or oil and drink? Is there anything wrong with wishing for your needs to be met—and desiring for them to be pleasing, attractive, or tasty? Is there anything wrong with wanting and needing clothes—and not just any old clothes but a nice wardrobe? Is there anything wrong with desiring pleasure—delicious food and refreshing drink, vacations and hobbies, or whatever else brings you pleasure? Is there anything wrong with wanting to be noticed by those around you?

No way! All of those things can be *good* things. Security, a healthy self-image, and satisfaction in life are not only good, but important. God wired you to want those things because He wants to give you those things. God created you to need those good things because ultimately they reveal that you need Him—the giver of those good things.

Did Hosea give Gomer shelter and security, clothes and comforts that brought her pleasure along with all the attention she desired? Absolutely! But Gomer wanted what she didn't have, not what she had. Though she had enough, it wasn't sufficient. When you *phroneo* on things below, you will never be satisfied.

When our hearts and minds aren't set on things above, when we haven't *phroneoed* (is that even a word?) on things above and allowed our heart's affection to be cemented in God's truth, we will overlook what we have and instead *phroneo* things below. It's just how we are.

So, think about what you go for.

What motivates you? Where do you find that buzz, that sense of identity, that attention or acceptance you desire? Circle the words that apply to you:

- Relationships
- Food
- Shopping
- Appearance
- Approval of others
- Career

- Kids
- Money
- Being morally good or admired
- Popularity

When you think about the things you gravitate toward—the things that influence you—are they instead of God or along with God? Really think about that!

Now, please be honest. You have nothing to hide. We Gomer girls all struggle with this even if we don't like to admit it.

What Women Aren't Saying

While we want our heart's affections to be set on things above, it's hard to resist the pull of things below, even though we don't want to feel it—and we sure don't want to admit it. I sense many of us Gomer girls aren't being real with ourselves—or with each other—and that's part of the problem.

The George Barna Group* did a massive survey of women who call themselves Christian—you know, women who find their security and identity in Christ. They examined their lifestyle, priorities, values, and commitments.

Barna found that when it comes to our personal relationship with God, only 1 percent of us confess that we are "usually not too close" or "feel extremely distant from God."

Wow! That means the rest of us claim to be extremely, really, or very close to God most of the time. Are you ever in that 1 percent? *Ever?!* When we are close to God, we don't stray from Him or forget

---

* Barna Group, "Christian Women Today, Part 2: What Women Want" (8/17/2012) and "Christian Women Today, Part 3: A Well-Being Check-Up" (8/21/2012), www.barna.org

who we are in Him. This means that most of us should be super secure, unshakable in our identity, and feeling completely accepted all the time. Do you believe this? Neither do I! So what gives?

Now, for that 1 percent (or perhaps more!) of us whose hearts stray from God from time to time, *phroneo* things below, and struggle with our sense of identity, we argue that we can't help it—we're influenced by outside forces.

But evidently we don't want to be honest about some of those influences either. At least that was the case with the women the Barna Group surveyed. We Christian women are more than willing to admit we're influenced by our faith. Of the women surveyed, 75 percent said that the Bible has influenced them "a lot," and 51 percent said the same thing about sermons. Most of these women were also quick to admit that their husbands have an impact on their actions and decisions—63 percent of married women reported that their husbands influence them "a lot."

But after those top three influencers—the Bible, sermons, and husbands—Christian women aren't quick to volunteer that they are swayed by outside voices. Only 10 percent of them said their friends have a significant impact on their decision making. And even fewer admitted that the media had any influence on them. Only—wait for it, wait for it!—5 percent said that the media influences them "a lot," 25 percent said that the media influences them "some," and a whopping 70 percent claimed that the media has "little" influence on their decision making.

Do I know these women? Are *all* of them really that secure in who they are? Am I to believe that they truly aren't easily influenced by voices that tell them they're a nobody and other voices that tell them how to become somebody?

Suddenly I felt like the only woman who was in Christ but still in crisis!

Evidently I'm not alone in this confusion. The president of Barna Group, David Kinnaman, was asked to explain why so few women say they are influenced by the media. Here's his reply: "In many ways, women's self-perception revealed in this study seems to be aspirational. Women want to be influenced by the Bible, but they reject the idea of being heavily affected by the media. So these aspirations may be reflected in the numbers. Still, the way women describe themselves reveals something: they seem to know how they want to be perceived by others."

When that smart guy explained those stats, I realized I wasn't the only woman who struggled with this. The sweet sisters who responded to the survey probably struggle too. They were just quick to give a "right" answer even if it wasn't an honest answer.

Now, I'm not saying these Christian women were being intentionally dishonest. Their answers reflect their best selves, their ideal, and I'm sure that on many days, they hit it. We all do. The Gomer girls who said, "No, I am more influenced by the Bible than by the media" may have really been saying, "I want to be more influenced by the Bible than by anything else." I want that too, don't you? Of course we want our minds and hearts set on things above. But the truth is we often hear other voices louder than we hear the truth of Scripture, and those voices can influence us. Have you heard some of the same voices I have?

- *You aren't smart enough.*
- *She's prettier than you are.*
- *If you're not perfect, you're not acceptable.*

- *If you perform well, you will be loved.*
- *You aren't thin enough.*
- *Nobody even notices you.*

What influences make you feel like somebody? What are you drawn to that helps you discover your identity? Where do you find your security when you feel invisible? If this is the first time you've thought about this, it may be hard for you to answer those questions. So ponder them as long as you need to until you get some clarity. Ask God, and His Spirit will show you.

To get free, we've got to get honest!

Honesty Brings Freedom

What we are not honest about, we will never be free from. And I know you want to be free—free to be the beloved.

I wonder how honest Gomer was with herself. She probably never acknowledged that she wasn't identifying with who she was according to her marriage covenant, and consequently, she didn't allow it to identify her. She didn't acknowledge her completeness as Hosea's wife, so she tried to complete herself. If we don't embrace the astounding truth that we are seen by God, we too will risk trying to get noticed in all the wrong ways. Gomer may have said "I do," but she was living "I'm not." *I'm not loved. I'm not special. I'm not happy. I'm invisible.*

The reality, though, could not have been further from the truth. Once she said "I do," she was no longer Gomer the harlot. She was Gomer the betrothed, the bride, the beloved wife. She didn't have to go anywhere to get her needs met. She didn't need to find herself but instead realize that she was already found.

How about you?

What do you already have in God that you are seeking in something or someone else? What have you not fully identified with in your true identity?

I'll tell you what I seek. A reminder of it sits on a shelf in my office, and on really vulnerable days, I keep it in the pocket of my purse so I can carry it with me wherever I go. It's an eight-letter word—eight Scrabble letters glued in place on a Scrabble game ledge. It might look like a cute little craft, but its meaning is beyond value.

Several years ago my friend Lisa texted me with a question: "If one word could become a reality in your life, what would it be?" When I texted her back, asking her to clarify, she responded, "You pick the word you most want as a reality in your life. Only you know what it means to you."

Girl, I have to say this took me a while! The one word that kept coming to my mind was "accepted," yet I kept pondering, too embarrassed to admit that "accepted" was without a doubt my word.

> Accepted is who we already are.
> Acceptance is what we already have.

Funny, isn't it? I was insecure enough to fear that my friend might reject me if she knew acceptance was what I longed for! Now,

Lisa is the most loving, accepting woman I know. My hesitation wasn't a reflection on her. It was a reflection on me and how much pressure I felt to be perfect in order to be accepted. My skewed belief was that I was acceptable only when I was impressive. Clearly I had not truly identified with my identity!

Accepted is who I already am. Acceptance is what I already have.

But acceptance is also what I seek—what I long for. Seeking acceptance is my way of saying, "I will go after my lovers who give me my wool and flax...bread and water...oil and drink...attention and identity."

Now that I've told you my word, think about what your own word might be. What is it that you already have in God that you're still seeking in other people or places? Try to narrow it down to just one word and then write it down.

Think of it this way: What if you constantly seek out food to make you happy? What is it that you're really seeking that you already have in God? Could your word be *satisfaction*?

Or suppose you feel a driving need to have perfect kids—perfectly dressed, perfectly behaved, perfectly talented—so you will look like the perfect mom. What is it that you already have in God that you're trying so hard to find? Could it be *admiration*?

Perhaps you feel invisible to your husband or to the other important people in your life. So you try hard—too hard—to make them notice you. What is it that you're after that you already have in God? Could it be undivided *attention*?

Have you decided on *your* word yet? If you own a Scrabble game, go ahead and pull out the letter tiles that spell your word and set them on the ledge so you can be reminded. My Scrabble word *accepted* always reminds me that I already have what I want.

When I am feeling less than acceptable, I hold it in my hand, wrap my fingers around it, and tell myself, "This is what God gave me. This is who I am."

Can you take that truth in?

If you feel invisible, it may be because deep down you never accepted that you are seen by God and have His full attention.

Just like Lisa glued the word *accepted* to a Scrabble ledge for me, ask God to glue your own word to your heart so that with every heartbeat, you feel the truth of it. Doing this will help you cement that truth in the ever-setting depth of your heart. If we don't remain close to the truth of who we are and what we have in God, we will stray from the truth and find ourselves enslaved by lies.

Gomer, of course, had trouble identifying with her new and true identity, going outside of her marriage to find her identity. She lost focus on Hosea, their marriage covenant, and who she was. And she quickly reverted back to her old self—Gomer the party girl, Gomer the prostitute. She neglected—and eventually rejected—who she was with Hosea and what she had in him and with him. And she sought out other lovers to give her something she already had. Surely their bread wasn't any tastier, was it? Their water wasn't any wetter. The thread count of the wool and flax they offered wasn't any higher than the fabric Hosea gave her. And their oil and drink? Those were probably cheaper and watered down! But Gomer wasn't thinking objectively.

Gomer did not have correct thinking, so she developed corrupt thinking.

We do the same thing, don't we? When we don't identify—on a daily basis—with our true identity, we forget who we are and who our First Love is, and we wander off to other lovers of acceptance and significance to get our needs met. We all need our bread and water, wool and flax, and oil and drink. It's just that we already have what we need in God. And what we don't feel we have received from Him, we become determined to achieve on our own. We trust ourselves and follow our own wisdom and way to get our needs met. As Hosea wrote, we, like Israel, "rejected what is good" (Hosea 8:3).

Put simply, we—like Israel and Gomer—don't act out of our identity. We act out of our *iddiction*.

Iddiction

Iddiction. The word isn't Greek, and it's not a typo. Let me explain.

When we Gomer girls have our heart's affection set on things below, we feel the dissatisfaction. We're painfully aware of our own insecurity and invisibility. We don't want those things to bother us. In fact, we'd like nothing better than to blow off those ugly urges! But we find our feelings hard to ignore because, truth be told, we're on our own minds—a lot. And we're drawn to anyone or anything that will give us the sense of self we lack. We're all a little Gomeristic. We're all *iddicts*.

An iddict is someone who finds her identity in herself rather than in God.

An iddict seeks her own way, elevates her own wants, and trusts ultimately in her own wisdom.

We become iddicts when we neglect or reject our true identity and God's wisdom and ways. We become iddicts when we go to "other lovers" like compulsive eating or compulsive shopping to meet our need for satisfaction. We become iddicts when we find our sense of worth in our career, our appearance, or our social media standing. We become iddicts when our children's behavior, our well-appointed homes, or our list of accomplishments make us feel like we're truly somebody. And we become iddicts when we do whatever we can—whatever it takes—to be accepted.

In other words iddicts look for their identity in themselves. That's what causes them to "go after their lovers." They neglect the true God for new gods they imagine will give them identity and significance.

That's just what Gomer did. She tried to find her identity in herself and her lovers when she stopped identifying with her new identity as a chosen, loved woman. I know a certain author, one who sat on a back deck overlooking a lake, who discovered she too was an iddict when she went after "other lovers" and tried to find acceptance, identity, and value in what others thought of her on social media.

Hello. My name is Jennifer, and I am an iddict!

I am addicted to *me*—my way, my wants, and my wisdom.

Yes, I certainly have days when I think that my way and my wants and my wisdom are enough. If life is good, I am good, and I don't need God for anything. But oh, girl! If I feel less than enough or insecure—if I gain weight or lose a friend—well, then my iddiction shows up because I've totally lost my sense of self.

As I read the book of Hosea over and over, I realize how much I am like Gomer—prone to wander and destined to end up just like her, leaving the one she loves only to find herself in a place she didn't want to be. Like Gomer, I am a chosen, loved woman. So why is my iddiction stronger than my identity?

Have you wondered the same thing?

You too are a chosen, loved woman. Do you identify with your identity? Or is your iddiction stronger than your identity? Really ponder these questions, my fellow Gomer girl. An iddict is forever begging God and others, "Accept me! Please accept me!" But because she seeks that acceptance in all the wrong places, all she feels is, "except me." *God loves everyone...except me. Everyone is so good...except me. Everyone is worthy...except me. Everyone is somebody...except me.*

The sad reality is iddicts believe lies.

Lies Iddicts Believe

Oh, Gomer girl, can't you see how important it is for us to identify with our true identity? Otherwise we live like iddicts, bent on finding ourselves and getting our needs met by all the wrong sources. And, naturally, the result is never good. Hosea 4:6 sums this up clearly: "My people are ruined because they don't know what's right or true" (MSG).

Yes, we iddicts tend to forget what is right or true. And that includes forgetting what is right or true about ourselves!

We iddicts often feel invisible because we overlook who we are and who God is.

An important thing to remember about iddiction is that it's not based on truth. Iddiction wouldn't remain—or even exist in the first place—if it didn't have lies to jump-start and fuel it. So let me share with you three lies that iddicts believe—lies I have believed—to help you see them for what they are: untruths that are not part of your true identity!

Lie #1: Who I am and what I struggle with are the same thing.

It might make sense to think, *If I fail, I am a failure.* But that's not true! Yes, we all make mistakes, but our struggles don't have to define us—they can *refine* us. God determines who we are, and our struggles can be used to clarify His life and character in us. If we assume that we are our weaknesses, we will live in defeat. We are who God says we are; we're not the culmination of our failures. You may *feel* rejected or unnoticed or nonproductive or...well, fill in your own word, but that doesn't mean you *are* any of those things. When you know who you truly are and act out of your correct identity, you should always begin with "I am..." instead of "I feel..." when you describe yourself. And then put in the correct word: *I am God's beloved. I am chosen. I am satisfied.*

> Our struggles don't have to define us—they can refine us.

Lie #2: Who I am and what I do are the same thing.

We are human *beings*, not human *doings*, aren't we, Gomer girl? Our identity is not based on what we do. It's based on what God did for us. If we base our sense of self on our abilities, our profession, or our status, we risk losing our sense of self when and if those things change. And that will only leave us feeling disoriented and wondering who we are. So instead, we must base our identity on that which never changes—the truth of God's Word and His everlasting love for us. We simply need to receive who we are from God, not achieve a status for God.

> Our identity is not based on what we achieve—it's based on what God did for us.

Lie #3: Who I am is not good enough.

When we are performance driven rather than provision driven, it enables us to live with a "not good enough" mentality. We tell ourselves that we must perform in order to be accepted, yet God tells us that He has already performed on our behalf—and His provision is sufficient. When we feel the need to be more, it's a reminder to *phroneo* on truth and realize that God is enough.

Unfortunately, iddicts tend to trust their opinion of themselves more than they trust God and His opinion of them. But there's one thing I do know for certain. My opinion on its own is not good enough to tell me the truth of who I am!

We tell ourselves we must perform
in order to be accepted,
yet God has already performed
on our behalf.

Gomer girl, let's help each other believe truth! When we know God's truth and believe God's truth, we are satisfied, set free from iddiction, return to our true identity, and find that we had what we were searching for all along. So instead of seeking satisfaction in the bread and water, wool and flax, and oil and drink of "other lovers," let's find our satisfaction in the Living Water and the Bread of Life!

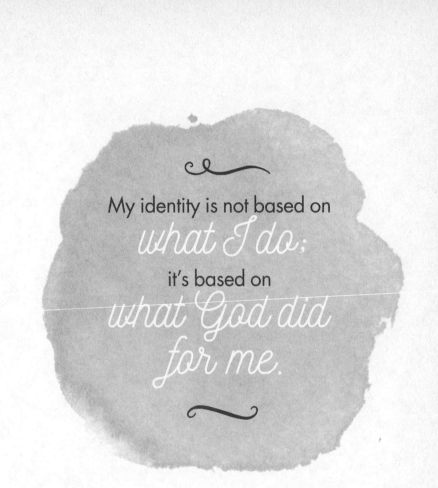

My identity is not based on
what I do;
it's based on
what God did for me.

#TheInvisibleBook

6

Gomerisms

*Ephraim (Israel) is oppressed, crushed in
judgment, because he was determined
to follow man's command.*

HOSEA 5:11 NASB

It happened on April 23, 1985. This was the day the 99-year-old
Coca-Cola company announced it was scrapping its original soda
formula for a newer, sweeter version. I know, I know! Sit down and
take a deep breath. This is some serious stuff here! (If you're from
the South like me, though, you will totally agree!)

For this southern girl, the new Coca-Cola was a big deal. You
don't mess with my Coke! In fact, I think my Coke-loving papa
used to pour the favorite soft drink right into my baby bottle. He
lived to be over 100 years old, and he credits part of his longevity
to drinking a glass bottle of Coca-Cola every day of his life. In fact,
I think the roots of my family tree were watered with Coke!

Coca-Cola was the leader of all soft drink companies with
skyrocketing sales. They had everything they could want in their

existing Coke formula. But they decided to overlook what they had in favor of creating something more, something better. So in the spring of 1985, they announced their new product—a sweeter formula that would replace the real thing. They called it the New Coke. It *was* sweeter—and it was a disaster!

After the New Coke made its debut, the Coca-Cola Company received thousands of complaint letters, numerous unhappy phone calls, and reams of bad press. And just three months after this national uproar, Coca-Cola announced the return of Coca-Cola Classic. This was such a big deal that ABC news anchor Peter Jennings actually interrupted the daytime soap opera *General Hospital* with the breaking news that the real thing was back. You just can't replace the real thing!

But we try, don't we? Oh, sister, we try!

When we feel invisible, that's when we feel like replacing God's way with our own way. And so we overlook God's wisdom and trust our own wisdom. We replace identity with iddiction. And when we do that, we practice *Gomerisms*. Yep, another new word just for us Gomer girls. *Gomerisms*.

I coined the word Gomerisms because it captures the essence of what Gomer did, what Israel did, and what we do—what all iddicts do—when we try to replace the Real Thing with our own thing. And because Gomer and Israel had so much in common, we can take a peek at the book of Hosea to see how the Israelites practiced Gomerisms.

The list is long! Israel's iddictive ways led the people to curse, lie, murder, steal, and commit adultery (Hosea 4:2). Along with that they chose to consult idols and listen to a diviner's rod (Hosea 4:12). And then there was the matter of their attitude—pride that caused them to stumble into sin (Hosea 5:5). They also chose to mix with other nations and be influenced by their evil ways when God had clearly called them to be set apart (Hosea 7:8). And finally, the Israelites decided to set up kings without God's approval and make—and worship—their own idols (Hosea 8:4).

Whew! Not a pretty picture, is it? Now, take another look at that list and circle the actions that apply to you. And then note what you did *not* circle. Chances are you didn't circle *murder* or *listen to a diviner's rod*. And you may not have circled *idol worship* or *mixing with foreign nations*. But let's bring the Israelite iddiction into today's world. Are there any things in our current culture that could be the equivalent of idol making and worship, consulting a diviner's rod, mixing with foreign nations, or demanding your own king?

Yes, life is different for us, but we make and worship idols when we take the things we own, the accomplishments we've achieved, or the people we admire and put so much emphasis on them that we actually make gods out of them. And when we give these things an unhealthy amount of focus, credit, or influence in our lives, we worship them.

What about consulting a diviner's rod? That happens when people let superstitions influence their actions or believe—and follow—their horoscopes. In fact, divining rods are all over TV. It's nearly impossible to channel surf without coming across someone urging you to consult a psychic or a medium. But you don't have to go to those extremes to consult a divining rod. What about placing your own intuition and your own feelings—faulty as they may be sometimes—over God's truth in your life?

And then there's the matter of mixing with other nations. God instructed the Israelites not to marry people from foreign nations because they worshipped idols. He didn't want His people to get confused and become unfaithful to Him. Today it's not a big deal if someone marries a person from another nation. But we *are* at risk when we become caught up with secular or worldly things that dilute our faith.

Finally, what about demanding your own king? Have you ever done that? In Israel's case God gave the people exactly what they wanted. They were so sure they wanted their own king—someone of their own choosing—and their own way. It wasn't God's best for them, but He allowed it to happen. And just look at Gomer. Well, it was pretty obvious what was king in her life, wasn't it? Her desire for lovers took priority over everything else. Now, what about you? Could demanding your own king be the same as demanding your own way above all else—your way or no way?

Those things represent what I call Gomerisms, and they always put us on the wrong path because they pull us away from the Real Thing and, instead, draw our attention to shallow substitutes. I like to put Gomerisms into three categories. First, *trusting in my own wisdom* is a Gomerism. Second, *elevating my own wants* is a Gomerism. And third, *demanding my own way* is a Gomerism.

Given what we've learned so far, Gomerisms appear to always hinder—not help—us in our quest to live out our true identity. But are Gomerisms *always* a bad thing?

What Is Right with Gomerisms

The root of a Gomerism isn't wrong. The root of a Gomerism represents the natural and expected longings of our human nature. But because we are prone to wander—and because correct thinking can so quickly become corrupt thinking—we can get terribly confused. We all deal with this confusion because we, like all sheep, can go astray. In fact, sometimes our wandering ways bring all the Gomerisms to the surface at once as we simultaneously trust in our own wisdom, elevate our own wants, and demand our own way. While the root of our desires and decisions isn't always wrong, the results can be disastrous.

Your Wisdom

Let's think about wisdom and what it means to trust in your own wisdom. God gave you a good mind, and He wants you to use it. And while it is right to consult your own wisdom, it's Gomeristic to trust solely in it. Proverbs 3:5-6 says, "Trust in the LORD with all your heart and do not lean on your own understanding. In all your ways acknowledge Him, and He will make your paths straight" (NASB).

God's Word clearly instructs us to trust Him above all else. When we consider our own wisdom equal to—or above—God's wisdom, we eventually choose our way over His way, and we follow in Gomer's footsteps.

Your Wants

We should acknowledge our wants, but it's Gomeristic to elevate our own wants above everything and everyone else. Here's what God's Word says on the matter: "Do nothing out of selfish ambition or vain conceit. Rather, in humility value others above yourselves, not looking to your own interests but each of you to the interests of the others" (Philippians 2:3-4).

Putting what we want above both other people's needs and

what God desires for us will only serve to make us more selfish. And the more *we* are on our own minds, the more self-aware and self-absorbed—and the less happy—we will be.

Your Way

It's reasonable to *desire* your own way, but it's Gomeristic to *demand* it. Why? Because God says His way—not your way—is perfect: "As for God, his way is perfect: The LORD's word is flawless; he shields all who take refuge in him" (Psalm 18:30).

God's way is guaranteed perfect; my way not so much. We just can't trust completely in our own hearts because it's so easy for our emotions to deceive us.

Your *wisdom.* Your *wants.* Your *way.* Which of these Gomerisms do you struggle with most? Which of them have caused you the most trouble—the most relational turmoil, the most spiritual stress, the most personal struggle?

Going for Our Gomerisms

We all have our own Gomerisms that the GPS of our soul navigates toward. Some of us focus on our own wisdom. We're smart and we know it, so why not use the brain God gave us? Many of us quickly elevate our wants. No matter the situation, we want what we want!

For me, demanding my own way is the Gomerism that tends to rear its ugly head and create trouble—especially in my marriage. Phil and I are opposites in many ways, but in one particular way we are exactly alike—we are both always right. Neither of us is ever wrong! What's more, we both always have the only right opinion. Naturally most of the time, we don't *share* that same opinion. But we both stubbornly cling to the belief that our way is the best way, and—funny how this works—his way and my way are rarely the same way!

I've gotten a little smarter over the years, so I don't always tell Phil every time I think his way is wrong. But deep down, I do think it. And deep down, I always expect to get my own way because I just *know* it's the best way. When I don't get it, I add that instance to an invisible list I keep in my heart. I used to be able to tell you everything on that list, but thankfully I've chilled quite a bit as I've matured, and quite honestly I also just can't remember things as well as I used to. Menopause stole most of my functioning brain cells! (Hey, maybe that's what that hard-to-lose belly fat is—brain cells!) And to tell you the truth, even if I could remember those things, I wouldn't really want to.

My way is not all it's cracked up to be. It's not always the best way, and it's certainly not the only way. But when I feel insecure or invisible, I will act out of my iddiction, pull out my favorite Gomerism, and start demanding my way. That's one of my methods for trying to feel seen, acknowledged, or accepted.

Like we always do, I substitute iddiction for identity.

When we act out of our true identity,
we're all about God's way.

When I keep that invisible list of times I didn't get my own way, I'm not acting out of my identity as a loved and chosen woman of God—a woman who can forgive and then give in. I am, instead, acting as an iddict and practicing my Gomerisms. But then there are those amazing times when I *do* act out of my identity and realize that my way just isn't all that important. When I act out of my identity, I am all about God's way of love and other-centeredness, and you can imagine how much better our marriage is in those moments!

So start to really notice which of your Gomerisms are showing up, when they tend to appear, and where they are doing the most damage. A good way to begin to identify them is by noticing the thought patterns that usually follow a Gomerism: *Ugh, I shouldn't have! Man, I wish I wouldn't have! Oh, if I just could have!* Put simply, you feel regret—regret about the things you did, the things you said, the choices you made.

You know it's a Gomerism when you wish you could rewind, redo, or erase.

So how can you avoid the "woulda, coulda, shoulda" of Gomerisms? Ask yourself three different questions before you take action: *Could I be wrong? Would I recommend?* and *Should I rethink?*

Could I Be Wrong?

Once you've identified the Gomerism—or Gomerisms—that are giving you the most trouble, stop yourself as soon as you recognize it. Depending on which Gomerism you're dealing with, ask yourself a good, hard question: *Could demanding my way right now be wrong? Could elevating my wants in this situation be wrong? Could trusting my own wisdom be wrong?* In short, you're asking yourself one simple thing: *Could I be wrong?* If your answer is anything but a definite—and emphatic—*no,* give yourself time before taking any action. You are never wrong to pause and assess your motivation or your actions.

Would I Recommend?

When you feel tempted to be Gomeristic, ask yourself if you would recommend your thoughts or your behavior to someone you love. Would you tell your child to behave the way you're tempted to behave at that moment? Would that behavior bring them peace and wholeness? Would you recommend that your boss or spouse act the way you're about to act? And if so, how would you like to be on the receiving end of that Gomerism? If you wouldn't recommend your thoughts, or your behavior, to someone else, chances are that you don't need to think or behave that way either! Then take a moment to reflect and pray. Ask God to remind you who you are so you can act out of your identity, not your iddiction.

Should I Rethink?

It's impossible to think before every single word you speak—*really* think through the ramifications of each individual word. But once you've identified which Gomerism you struggle with, you can put your brain and your heart on high alert to be aware of thinking before you say—or do—something you regret.

If you realize that in certain settings or with certain people you tend to act out of your iddiction (such as when you're with people who push all your insecurity buttons), be prepared to rethink your thinking! Tell yourself, *I will rethink so I won't regret.* Rethink why you insist on demanding your own way if that's your Gomerism. Rethink why you elevate your wants higher than anything else if that's your Gomerism. Rethink why it is that you trust ultimately in your own wisdom if that's your Gomerism. It's easy to go on mental autopilot if we've been on a wrong path in the past, and, of course, that mental autopilot will take us back to the same old place. So ask yourself, *Should I rethink?* And the answer to that, most of the time, is *yes*! Rethink!

Shift from *My* to *Thy*

As you begin to recognize your favorite Gomerisms, ask God to help you start making the shift from acting out of your iddiction to acting out of your identity. A helpful way to see if you're heading for a Gomerism is to replace the word "my" with "Thy." Yeah, I know, "Thy" is a King James kind of word, but it rhymes nicely with "my," so it's easy to remember.

> The more we act out of our identity,
> the sooner "my" and "Thy" will
> become the same thing.

I'm using "Thy" to represent God. When the Gomer in you starts to wander off her own way, stop and remind yourself that you will not give in to your iddiction. Say out loud, *I choose Thy way over my way, Lord. I choose Thy wisdom over my wisdom, Lord. I choose Thy wants and desires over my wants and desires, Lord.*

The really cool thing here is that the more you act out of your identity, the sooner "my" and "Thy" become the same thing. In other words God's way becomes your way. God's wants become your wants. And God's wisdom becomes your wisdom. I love that!

Your iddiction starts to lose its power because you aren't feeding it with as many lies, and you will become more confident in your true identity.

Gomerisms encourage us to wander, and they never take us where we want to go. They never lead us to be who we really want to be—who we already are in Christ. Gomerisms also pull us farther away from our Source of self—God Himself. And remember what happens when we leave our Source of self? We lose our sense of self!

So go, go, go away, Gomerisms. You ain't welcome here no more!

The very last verse in the book of Hosea says, "If you want to live well, make sure you understand all of this. If you know what's good for you, you'll learn this inside and out. God's paths get you where you want to go. Right-living people walk them easily; wrong-living people are always tripping and stumbling" (Hosea 14:9 MSG).

Gomer girl, God's paths *do* get us where we want to go. And they lead us to be who we are—the beloved.

Now, let me tell you one thing before we finish this chapter. When I first stumbled on this thing I call iddiction, I was bummed. I thought, *I should know better! I should be past this!* I was frustrated and ashamed that what I thought was low self-esteem was really high self-awareness—self-absorption, actually. And when I realized that the times I felt the most invisible were usually the times I

was the most self-absorbed and completely acting out of my iddiction, I was embarrassed.

Nobody wants to think they're selfish. I want to think I've
grown less selfish as I've grown closer to God. And I have. But as
long as I live on this earth, there will always be some iddiction in
me. The problem is at first it's hard to know what to do with it or
how to change it. I know that I had no clue what to do! Sure, I'd
started to identify lies and *phroneo* on truth, but it wasn't a quick
fix. And while there may not be a quick fix, there is a process that
really does work.

If you're starting to see that the times you feel the most invisible
are the times you are the most self-absorbed, and if you're realizing that your low self-esteem could actually be high self-awareness,
please be patient with yourself and the process. This is not a problem we need to fix. It's a tension we learn to manage.

Because iddicts live with that big letter "I," we can be quick to
condemn ourselves: *"I" am such a loser. "I" am not good enough. "I"
will never amount to anything.*

But try not to let the "I" in iddiction speak too loudly, sweet
Gomer girl. After all, "I" is smack-dab in the middle of *lie*.

Instead, let your "I" be found where it should be—hidden in
Chr-i-st!

In Christ is where your true identity is found. And that is the
one place you are never, ever invisible!

7

Faulty Bow Syndrome

They do not turn to the Most High;
they are like a faulty bow.

HOSEA 7:16

As Little League parents, Phil and I had our game-day routine down. We'd set up our chairs, unfold the blankets, and pull our drinks out of the cooler. On this particular day, we were set up on the sidelines of Little League field number four, prepared to watch the Defenders—our son's team—face the Hornets. We were feeling pretty comfortable until a fellow team parent walked by and let us know that we were at the wrong field!

"We'll just sit here while the boys warm up, and then we'll move," Phil said.

As we were chatting, I heard someone near me fiddling with a chair. "May I sit here?" a woman asked.

"Sure," I said, "but we're only going to be here a few more minutes. We're at the wrong field."

As if she hadn't heard a word I said, the woman began, "My name is Mavis. My husband is a scorekeeper, so I spend lots of time on the ball field."

I offered a polite, "Hmmm..." as Mavis continued. And what ensued was a brief—or perhaps not-so-brief!—history of all things Mavis. She told me where she was from, how many siblings she had, where she was in the birth order—and why she liked it. I also found out what her parents did for a living, when they died, how she met her husband, the names of her children—and their spouses as well as their pets. I even discovered her favorite dessert. Whew! But that wasn't all. By the time Mavis had finished, I knew her preferred laundry soap brand as well as her favorite bra designer. Seriously!

I must admit I wasn't sorry when it was time to move to the other ball field. Mavis was a sweet lady, but man, she was a little too chatty and self-absorbed for my taste.

Mavis had been draining, and I was already running on empty. I'd had a hectic week, and my agenda for the day at the ball field didn't even include paying attention to the game. No, my agenda was made pretty obvious by the stuff in my bag—my latest iPhone download (a C.S. Lewis audiobook) and some decadent dark chocolate. I was plotting to sneak in my earbuds, hide the dark chocolate under my blanket, and stare at the Defenders on the field all the while listening to *Reflections on the Psalms*. I'd even schemed to clap when Phil clapped and whoop and howl when he did so I could hide what I was really doing!

And then I heard a familiar voice: "I brought my craft bag." The next thing I knew, Mavis was setting her chair next to ours and telling us we "looked crafty." When Phil chuckled, she reprimanded,

"You're the age of my son. He's not too old to do crafts with his mother, and neither are you."

With that pronouncement she passed my almost-50-year-old, Ph.D. husband some tissues. "We're going to make babies in a blanket," she explained with total seriousness. "My uncle Seth used to do this with a real handkerchief. Did I tell you he was my favorite uncle? He was in the army..."

I couldn't believe it! So much for spending my afternoon listening to C.S. Lewis, nibbling dark chocolate, and getting some much-needed "me" time.

Step by step, Mavis explained how to fold the tissues. We followed along, and within several minutes we each held a tissue paper baby in a blanket. Then she said, "Oh, pardon me, sometimes I just break out in song." Seriously! She really said that. And then she demonstrated: "He's still working on me..." The old tune bellowed from deep in her soul.

Mavis nudged my elbow. "You know it, don't you?" How did she know that I knew it? But I did. I'd learned it as a girl growing up in church.

"Sing with me!" Mavis insisted. And so I sang with her.

My new friend was positively gleeful that she had found a singing buddy. I, on the other hand, was positively embarrassed as Phil discreetly whispered, "People are watching." Swallowing my pride, I tried to focus on Mavis rather than on myself, thinking that the song was almost over. But then she immediately dove into another gospel hymn. *Great*, I thought. *I know that one too.* Mavis pressed her elbow against mine again as if to say, "Keep singing!" So I did.

I couldn't believe I was singing a gospel duet with a flamboyant, slightly off-pitch, very loud stranger at the Little League field. But something in me had begun to soften. Something about the song lyrics and the way Mavis sang them so sincerely made me realize which of the two of us was the self-absorbed and self-centered one that day—and it wasn't Mavis.

The Paradox of Hedonism

Throughout that day at the ball field, one of Mavis's songs kept running through my mind: "The Longer I Serve Him."

It's true. The longer I serve God, the sweeter life grows, and everything becomes better and better as He becomes my focus.

But that sentiment does not apply to my self-serving tendencies. The longer I serve *me*, the worse things get and the more bitter, insecure, discontent, and self-centered I become. When it's all about me—my wisdom, my wants, and my ways—the less sweet life is.

Think of our girl Gomer. She served herself, didn't she? She left Hosea for other lovers, expecting to get something bigger and better. But did she?

Gomer operated according to a basic reality of human experience that we can all relate to. Philosophers call it the *paradox of hedonism*. Ever heard of it? Even if you haven't, you've lived it. I sure have. We all have.

The paradox of hedonism is also called the pleasure paradox. It's a concept in ethics that says pleasure cannot be acquired directly; it can only be acquired indirectly. In other words, the harder you try to find happiness, the further from you happiness goes. Or the more you try to serve yourself, the more dissatisfied you become.

William Bennett expressed it this way: "Happiness is like a cat. If you try to coax it or call it, it will avoid you. It will never come. But if you pay no attention to it and go about your business, you'll find it rubbing against your legs and jumping into your lap." That's a *purr-fect* example, isn't it? (I know. Sorry! I couldn't resist.)

When I am focused on me and myself, what I want and who I am, I will never be satisfied. Hosea captured the concept like this: "They will eat but not be satisfied; they will be promiscuous but not multiply; for they have abandoned their devotion to the LORD" (Hosea 4:10 HCSB).

Put simply, the end result of iddiction is not satisfaction; it's an empty, unhappy identity crisis.

Operating as a Faulty Bow

Like all of us iddicts, Gomer was aiming for satisfaction, but she ended up landing in lack. And it's all because she was determined to follow her own way, elevate her own wants, and trust solely in her own wisdom.

Gomer was like a faulty bow. And when we practice Gomerisms—when we are set on serving ourselves—we are too. I bet you've never been called a faulty bow before, have you? Well, let me do a little explaining.

Hosea compares Israel—and us—to a faulty bow: "They do not turn to the Most High; they are like a faulty bow" (Hosea 7:16). It's a poetic way of saying we are misguided and therefore unreliable.

When we are functioning as a faulty bow, we are bent our own way. We shoot our arrows of desire, hoping they hit our intended target. But they never do.

A faulty bow believer is bent on her own way and wisdom. As a result, her arrows don't land in the right places.

When we're operating as a faulty bow, we long for identity, but we land in crisis. We shoot for pleasure, but we end up requiring more and more to make us happy. We target acceptance, but we hit greater insecurity. We long to be seen and acknowledged, but we end up feeling jealous, envious, and invisible. Do you see what I mean? We aim for the right thing, but our arrow lands in the wrong place, and we find ourselves stuck in a difficult situation. Kind of like poor Gomer—she aimed for satisfaction, but she'll eventually land in slavery.

We often make choices or act in ways that seem fine at first but then end up making us feel ashamed or stuck. Let's say you like to shop. You feel happy and fulfilled when you buy the things you want, but then you can't pay the bills. Or you start to feel guilty about spending so much on things you don't really need, so you hide your receipts and purchases. If you're married and tell your husband how much money you spent, you make sure to round the number down. You justify your spending. Suddenly the thing that made you feel free—shopping—has made you feel enslaved. What gave you a buzz is now giving you shame. You have become a faulty bow.

Here's another example most of us girls can relate to. We feel that buzz of freedom when we eat. Our favorite foods make us feel powerful, happy, or comforted. So we nibble, munch, pig out— and we gain weight. Embarrassed, we try to eat less, but we begin to feel powerless. The pull is just too great, and so we start eating in secret. We hide dark chocolate in the underwear drawer. We stash Cheetos in the guest room closet. The result? Weight gain and shame (#trueconfession).

Suddenly, what at first made us feel free is now making us feel enslaved. We didn't get what we aimed for. We got something else entirely.

Hosea perfectly summarized what happens to us when we're like faulty bows: "They sow the wind and reap the whirlwind" (Hosea 8:7). We get a whole lot more than we bargained for, but none of it is what we originally set out to get.

Your desires aren't usually wrong. They just go wrong when you're a faulty bow.

Imagine it this way. God is the Master Archer. You are the bow in His hands. Just as an archer places arrows in a bow, God places desires, longings, drives, callings, and giftings in you. A desire for pleasure—like enjoying food or shopping—is a normal, healthy desire. A longing for acceptance is a natural part of being human. A drive to be your best, or do your best, is a God-given drive. But when we're a faulty bow, those desires go haywire. If we are bent out of shape because we're bent on our own way, what happens when the archer starts to shoot those arrows? That's right! They don't fly like they're supposed to, and they don't land where the archer intended. And so our giftings go astray, and we remain unfulfilled. In other words, the longer we serve ourselves, the more bent out of shape our bow becomes.

Do you ever look at your life and think, *How did I get here? When did I become this self-absorbed? How come I'm so insecure? Why do I always feel invisible? Why can't I ever feel good enough?* Maybe, Gomer girl, it's because you have become a faulty bow bent on your own way, and it's landed you in a place you never intended. So look at where you're standing right now. And while you're thinking about where your arrows have landed, consider whether or not that place is a minefield.

Maneuvering Through Minefields

The first place a faulty bow can send an arrow is into the mine-field of *competitiveness*. We're all driven to do well and to be acknowledged for our efforts. But when we act out of our iddic-tion instead of our identity, our arrows end up in the minefield of competitiveness. You know how this kind of thinking goes. *If she is good, I have to be better. If she is cute, I have to be cuter. If she has 158 Facebook friends, I need 159—actually 160 in case I lose one and then I'll still be ahead!*

Spelled out like this, it sounds silly, but you get the idea. When we don't feel complete in Christ, we compete with others. But we don't need to do this. Gomer girl, you are not a faulty bow. You're a faithful bow! So if you're tiptoeing through a minefield of com-petitiveness, try this...

Compliment Instead of Compete

Begin complimenting the women you are secretly competing against. Compliment someone for that quality in her that you're actually jealous of. Instead of thinking, *I hate you because you're so skinny*, say, "You really have a nice figure." Even if you never speak a word to the woman you've found yourself competing against, you can think complimentary thoughts about her every time that jeal-ous feeling starts to creep into your mind.

You're aiming for personal peace and a healthy sense of self-esteem, aren't you? Well, if you're constantly competing, you won't get what you're aiming for. But when you choose to compliment instead of compete, you will actually begin to like yourself. You'll feel magnanimous for your kindness rather than mad at yourself for being petty. When you make that shift from competing to complimenting, your faulty bow transforms into a faithful bow and you find yourself where you want to be—comfortable with yourself and happy for others.

> Turn competitiveness
> into compliments.

Encourage Instead of Envy

The next minefield to watch out for is in the territory of *envy*. Lots of us Gomer girls experience envy even if we don't often admit this. I sure don't want to admit to all the times I've felt envy because I don't like what envy says about me. I feel ashamed when I'm envious of another woman. It's a hard thing to love a friend so much, yet, at the same time, fight against feeling envious of her. And it's even worse when we allow that envy to morph into just plain dislike or even resentment.

It's also possible that you think you don't like someone at all when deep down all you are is jealous of her. Sometimes when we are extra critical or resentful of someone, it's because we are envious of her. And the main thing this reveals is that we really don't like ourselves very much.

Here's the deal: Envy of a friend is really a symptom of insecurity and discontentment with yourself. And who would dare to set up house on that minefield? No, thank you! If you find yourself constantly fighting feelings of jealousy, it's a clue that you may be operating as a faulty bow, misguided and unreliable.

Remember, being envious will always make you more self-aware and insecure, not less.

An envious person might say something like this: "I can't believe *she* got picked to do that job! She thinks she can do everything better than anyone else." What's really being said here is this: "I wish *I* had been chosen to do that job. I feel invisible because she got all the attention. And I'm filled with feelings of jealousy—not joy—toward her. Not only do I want her job, I also want all the attention and accolades she received for doing it so well."

Unattractive, right? None of us Gomer girls intends to live in envy of others, but when it happens (and it's bound to!) our thoughts can become downright ugly. And when we start to think this way, we're the only ones who lose. We lose joy and confidence and contentment as we grow in bitterness and anger and self-awareness. So how do you pick up that arrow, reset your bow, and get out of the minefield of envy? How do you stop your jealous thought patterns and put a halt to feelings of negativity?

By encouraging! Say, "Way to go! You did a terrific job!" When you offer this kind of pure, no-strings-attached encouragement, you'll feel so much better. You'll develop a pure heart and a kind spirit—things that are actually worth envying! Being encouraging to others is a beautiful way to serve the Lord. And the more you serve Him, the less you will serve yourself. Your character will grow, and your pettiness will shrink.

Turn envy into encouragement.

Thank Instead of Threaten

If you find yourself becoming overly sensitive or easily threatened, chances are good that you're a faulty bow. You aimed for the landscape of significance, but you've landed in the area of not-good-enough.

When you rest in the hand of God, the Master Archer, you never need to feel less than. But it's hard not to think about how others have treated us, and then we start to feel threatened. Maybe you weren't shown the respect you thought you deserved. Perhaps you feel like someone is out to get you or others never treat you the way you'd like to be treated.

If you interpret every suggestion as a slap in the face, every correction as a criticism, and every insight shared with you as an insult to your intelligence, chances are you're standing on a minefield—and it's exploding every minute!

So when you start to feel threatened, choose to be thankful instead.

How do you do this? Instead of taking everything personally, immediately take it to Jesus with a thankful heart. Say, *"Thank You, Lord, for teaching me and helping me grow."*

If you're threatened by someone you're a tad jealous of, thank

God for your friend's good attributes. She is who God made her to be, and so to resent what is good in her is to resent what God has done in—and for—her. This might be difficult to do, but it's so important. I know that when I'm not being who I am in God's hands—when I'm focusing on what I'm not—I can never be satisfied with myself, my life, or anything else. I am threatened by others because I'm not thankful for them—and I'm not thankful for me.

> When we're truly thankful,
> we won't feel threatened.

When we thank God for what He has done in—and for—someone else, our focus shifts from who we wish we were to who God is! When we look to Him, we find ourselves.

Competitiveness, envy, and feeling threatened are just a few of the minefields where faulty bows send their arrows.

Oh, Gomer girl, the real estate is endless!

Do you too struggle with Faulty Bow Syndrome? If you do—and we all do—ask God to show you where you are, and then hand your faulty bow to Him because being our own archer never, ever works. When we forget we are in the hands of the Master Archer, we start shooting ourselves into the center of everything so we can be seen and feel important. As C.S. Lewis wrote, "The moment you have a self at all, there is a possibility of putting yourself first—wanting to be the center."

When we put ourselves first, we risk having pride take over and bring us to our eventual dead end—a crash landing. As Proverbs 16:18 wisely says, "Pride goes before destruction, a haughty spirit before a fall."

God doesn't create faulty bows. If we choose to accept our identity as a loved, accepted, and complete woman of God, we will rest in the hands of the Master Archer. We will conform to His will and His ways, and we won't twist and turn and bend and posture to get our own way.

When we are a faithful bow, we'll be comfortable with the imperfect us—comfortable in the skin we're in.

I want to rest in the hands of the Master Archer, don't you? I want to rest in Him and in who He made me to be. I want to rest in His provision and His plan.

My friend, you too are a beautiful bow in His hand. He aims. You respond.

It's so much easier, so much more fulfilling, to rest in Him rather than recreate ourselves. That will only result in us getting bent out of shape and ending up in places we never wanted to go.

And if—well, *when*—you find yourself taking matters into your own hands and ultimately landing your arrows in the place you don't want to be, tell yourself, *You are not a faulty bow. You are a faithful bow!*

At the Little League field that spring morning, chatty Mavis made me sing "The Longer I Serve Him," and I am so glad she did! But the other song we sang in our ball field duet was "He's Still Working on Me." And He is. The beautiful thing, Gomer girl, is that He—God—works in us both "to will and to work for *His* good pleasure" (Philippians 2:13 NASB).

When we put our own feelings and our own thoughts first, we have nothing. But when we rest content in the capable hands of the Master Archer—when we allow Him to bend us His way—we have everything.

8

The Intervention

Therefore, behold, I will hedge up her way with thorns, and I will build a wall against her so that she cannot find her paths. She will pursue her lovers, but she will not overtake them; and she will seek them, but will not find them. Then she will say, "I will go back to my first husband, for it was better for me then than now!"

HOSEA 2:6-7 NASB

Our Gomer girl has been a gone girl. It's been months (at least a few chapters) since anybody has seen her in church. Everyone knows she's been having an affair. Hosea doesn't say anything about it, but he's probably the only one in the entire church who isn't talking about the scandal. When Gomer first disappeared, you tried to get in touch with her, but now you've stopped emailing and texting—you got the hint. She's not responding. She's not interested in talking to anyone from church.

You also used to see Gomer in the carpool line dropping her

kids off at school. Now it's Hosea you see every morning in his van in the lineup in front of you. Seeing his kids hop out of the van, you notice that Jezreel's clothes don't match, and his backpack has papers spilling out of it. Little Lo-Ruhamah's hair looks a mess as she trails behind her big brother. *Daddies just don't know how to do little girls' hair*, you think.

The buzz of your cell phone pulls you out of your thoughts. When you see who's calling, you hesitate before answering. It's your super chatty friend who...Well, let's just say she likes to talk—a lot. But you decide to go ahead and answer before heading home.

You put your Starbucks skinny, no-whip mocha into the cup holder and pick up your phone to say hello, but you barely get the word out before your friend starts in: "Oh, you won't believe this!" she exclaims. "I heard from my neighbor who heard from her husband that Gomer was at that club—you know, that sleazy one downtown where all those women—the kind of women like Gomer—hang out? I mean, sorry, I'm not being ugly. I'm just being honest. You know that place?"

Your friend barely stops for air as you roll your eyes and attempt an answer. Then she charges on. "Anyway, my neighbor's husband is sort of sleazy himself, so I'm not a bit surprised *he* was there. He saw Gomer there the other night, and she was with a man. And oh, my gosh, not just *any* man! She was with this guy—at least that's what my friend's husband said—who was covered in tattoos and looked like he was in the Mafia. Can you believe that? I guess Gomer and this guy were laughing and drinking and— Oh, girl! I can't even repeat what I heard Gomer had on or shall I say did *not* have on!"

Your friend emphasizes the word *not* with the same drama as a cat coughing up a hairball. You try to break in while she catches her breath. "Was she—" But you aren't fast enough.

"I just can't believe she left Hosea!" your chatty (um...gossipy?) friend exclaims. "She apparently doesn't look good either. You know if a man—especially a guy like my neighbor's husband—notices that a woman like Gomer doesn't look good, she must look awful."

She pauses, and you try again. "Oh, man, poor dear Gomer..." you begin.

"Stop talking to your sister like that!" you hear your friend erupt at her son on the other end. "Is that how the Bible says we should treat each other?"

"Uh," you continue, "I wonder if Gomer is okay. I mean can she really be happy?"

"Okay?" your friend scoffs. "Heavens no, she's not okay! She's a wreck—she's lost it! I can't believe a pastor's wife would act like that. And happy? She'd better not be happy. She should be wearing sackcloth, not Saks Fifth Avenue!"

"Really?" you question.

"Uh..." your friend begins to backpedal. "Well, yeah, poor Gomer. Like you said, poor Gomer. Um...bless her heart. I was just calling to say that we need to pray for her. Oh, gotta go. I have another call..."

Wow! After listening to your friend's lengthy "prayer request"—that piece of gossip she tried to play off as a spiritual concern—your ear hurts. Your heart hurts too. While part of you is frustrated with Gomer because she knew better than to leave her family and behave like this, part of you feels sorry for her because she's obviously been deceived and must feel miserable.

Poor Gomer, you think. *What has she gotten herself into?* You take a sip of your coffee and ask yourself, *Has she really ended up where she wanted to be?*

That's the question, isn't it? Has Gomer really ended up where she wanted to be? Is she truly happy in her current situation?

When you follow your Gomerisms, ignore your identity, and act out your iddiction, do you end up where you want to be? And are you happy there?

Or do you start to feel the ache of dissatisfaction and that familiar feeling of discontent?

When I start to notice a nagging discontent, or when I spend too much time comparing myself to someone else, it's a good indication that I have shifted from being a faithful bow to acting like a faulty bow.

I've struggled with feeling guilty and getting mad at myself when I find I've landed my arrows in a minefield. But instead of beating myself up, I'm learning instead to ask God to forgive me and then use that as a pathway to a better place rather than staying stuck in a dead end. And He's always faithful to do that for me. He can take your bad feelings about yourself—whether they're based on your own sin or just on a shaky self-image—and use all that negativity to bring about a very positive outcome.

Those bad feelings can be transformed into something good, which is what happens when God works one of His miraculous interventions.

The Intervention

If someone you love is battling a true addiction, sometimes what that person needs most is an intervention. Often, in fact, an intervention is the most loving thing you can do for someone who's trapped in a bad situation. But intervention ain't pleasant, is it? Most people don't willingly volunteer for a process where they will have to confront everything they don't like about themselves and come to terms with all the ways they need to change. But that kind of confrontation can actually be a conduit to freedom.

Gomer girl, I am an iddict. And every iddict needs an intervention.

If we are to be women who really understand just how incredibly loved and valued we are, an intervention may be just what we need.

Gomer sure needed one, and we'll soon discover that a slave block became that for her. Now, I doubt that our intervention will look like a slave block. But what do you suppose it could look like?

Thorns

God provides interventions for those whom He loves—and that means you and me. He did it for Israel, His beloved people, by allowing them to be oppressed and, eventually, attacked by their enemies. Doesn't sound very appealing, does it? But interventions sometimes come in not-so-pretty packages.

One of these packages might resemble a tangle of thorns: "Therefore I will block her path with thornbushes; I will wall her in so she cannot find her way" (Hosea 2:6).

In this verse God was telling the Israelites that He would block their way with thorns, enclosing them with a wall and obscuring their paths. They were going to experience quite the intervention as a consequence of their own poor decisions, but this intervention would be for their own good.

Have you ever gotten tangled up in thorns? You might be able to find your way through them eventually, but the process sure slows you down, cuts you up, and makes you think twice, doesn't it?

When God intervenes He might block our path of wayward wandering with thorns. It might be a prickly, painful conflict that we get tangled up in—seriously sharp thorns that God uses to get our attention and show us that we were made for more.

Can you think of an area in your life where you frequently find yourself caught in a tangle of thorns? Maybe it's a relationship with someone else—a family member, a friend, a coworker—where conflict constantly arises. Now, I know it's difficult, but try to think of that conflict as thorns that are actually helping you to slow down and forcing you to think twice about your actions.

One of my friend's daughters—I'll call her Lola for this story—is in constant conflict with her mother. I know this because I recently spent the day with them and heard Mom's version of it in my right ear and Lola's version in my left ear! Of course, each reported identical details yet with very different interpretations and reactions. Now, neither of them are perfect—not by a long shot. But I've got to say poor Lola creates a lot of the conflict because of her interpretation of her mom's words.

When Mom says, "Lola! You need to turn off your phone. It's 10:00, and the rule is your phone goes off at 10," Lola explodes. "That's not fair!" she shouts. "My friend Lulu gets to keep hers on until 10:30!"

Mom responds, "Well, I'm not Lulu's mom. I'm *your* mom, and this is our rule!"

You can probably imagine what happens next. "You don't trust me!" Lola shouts. "You're trying to control me! I can't stand you! I wish I lived at Lulu's house!"

Now, why is Lola tangled in thorns? Is it because her phone is supposed to be turned off at 10:00? Is it because she didn't turn it off on time? Is it because her mom told her to turn it off? Is it because Lulu has a perfect mother who Lola would be much, much happier living with? Is it because Lola's life would totally change if she could keep her phone on for an extra 30 minutes every night?

No, the thorny tangle happened because of Lola's iddiction. *My way! My wisdom! My wants!* Lola created her own sticky situation. She got tangled in conflict with her mom not because of her iPhone but because of her "I"—in other words because of her selfishness.

After hearing the whole sordid story, I gently asked Lola to think about the thorny tangle where she was constantly finding herself trapped. "Lola, do you *really* want this?" I asked. "Is it working for you? Is it bringing you peace?"

Lola pouted, but she saw where I was going. "Nope," she said.

I then explained to her that she could choose to see that conflict as a dead end in her relationship with her mom, or she could instead let it serve to slow her from stomping down a path of future unhappiness. The thorny conflict became an intervention because it gave Lola a chance to consider where she was heading and to see if she really liked that destination. She didn't, and she's currently trying to be more introspective than explosive when it comes to potentially prickly conversations with her mom.

Way to go, Lola!

What about your thorns? Think about how God can use them as an intervention in your life to slow you from traveling at lightning speed down a path that will destroy you or your relationships.

In fact, please take a moment here to pause with me and pray about this. It's so important, Gomer girl! Ask God to give you the grace to thank Him for those thorns and to teach you how to detangle when you find yourself stuck in them.

Walls

Hosea said that God would erect a barrier to slow down the people He loved: "I will wall her in so that she cannot find her way" (Hosea 2:6).

Have you ever experienced a wall from God that blocked your way? Forget about slowing down and thinking twice. A wall forces you to come to a screeching stop right where you are! I've had this happen, and I can guarantee that it's pretty painful to bang your head into a wall of your own making. But boy, does it help you avoid that path in the future!

I ran into a doozy of a wall early on in my ministry career. I had been invited by a large church's single adult ministry to sing at their New Year's Eve party. They wanted me to "sing in the New Year," which sounded like fun at the time. In retrospect, though, saying yes to this engagement was a bad, bad idea.

I was there to perform, but the crowd wasn't there to listen to a 20-something married blind woman sing. They were there to meet other 20-something eligible singles! And who would expect them to sit there and listen to me sing when they could be mingling, chatting, flirting, laughing, and playing games? Well, *I* expected them to listen!

So they chatted and mingled while I stood and sang. And here's what was really awkward. For some reason I thought that all of my songs—yep, *all* of them—required introductions, so I spoke between each and every song I sang. Of course, no one stopped their socializing to listen to me. And instead of having the maturity to adjust to the setting, I plowed on singing a song, introducing the next number, singing a song, and so on.

Not surprisingly—given my ridiculous expectations—with every song and ignored introduction, I was growing more and more frustrated. I thought that my audience was being rude, and I was offended. I thought I was mad at the audience, but my anger was just a mask of the insecurity I wore that night.

Anger is often a mask our insecurity wears.

What came next is one of the biggest regrets of my whole life—especially my ministry life. As soon as I finished my last song, I huffed to the oblivious audience, "Okay, I'm done now. You can stop talking over me."

You can imagine the sarcasm in my tone as I spoke those loving and mature words. Well, they did stop talking and listened—finally (#badtiming)!

In fact, they were silent.

I couldn't believe I'd actually said that. It was so rude. I was so rude! The singles minister, sensing disaster, quickly bounded on stage and enthusiastically thanked me while the stunned audience quietly clapped. It was incredibly awful, and it only took about three seconds for me to hear my own words echo in my heart: *You can stop talking over me.* Had I really just said that out loud?

Phil followed the minister on stage to walk me off just as the countdown to midnight began.

Ten! Nine! Eight!

"What did you just say?" my husband whispered as we descended the stairs.

Seven! Six! Five!

"Exactly what you thought I said," I moaned.

Four! Three! Two! One!

"Happy New Year!" is what Phil shouted at the same time as everyone else.

Yeah, happy New Year, I thought grimly.

I think we sold two CDs that night—one to the singles minister and one to the hearing-impaired gentleman who kept telling me I had a nice smile. In record time we packed our boxes and left. And I cried the entire three-hour drive home.

That painful experience became one of God's most important interventions in my life. Sure, it felt like a wall—the Great Wall of Jennifer—when I crashed into it. It sent me sprawling onto a giant mirror that showed me exactly who I was deep inside.

I was terribly insecure to begin with, but the experience of being overlooked and ignored exposed my vulnerability even more. However, the wall I hit that New Year's Eve did not become a dead end for me because God's grace allowed me to slowly but surely scale it. And on the other side of the wall, I found a pathway that led me to a place of humility where I was able to find my security in God—not in the attention (or lack thereof) and opinion of others. That wall was a gift of love from God to me.

Thorns and walls are never pleasant, and I bet they aren't what generally come to mind when you think of symbols of love, are they? Not for me! When I think of symbols of love, I think of flowers, dark chocolate, hugs, and kisses—not thorns and walls! But the thorns and walls remind us that God sees us, values us, and loves us. He loves us enough to slow us down and draw us back to Himself.

Thankfully, God is not an enabler of our iddictive behavior. He loves us too much! True, He sometimes throws barriers our way, but He does this out of protection and love for us. When He plants thorns in the avenue, a dangerous turnpike can become a turnaround.

Remember, if you feel like your faulty bow has launched your arrows into a difficult dead end or a prickly place, you might be feeling the sweet touch of God's love and mercy on your life. And the thorns and walls are the hands of God pushing against you—resisting you.

God Resists to Restore

In the New Testament, both James and Peter quote Proverbs 3:34 to tell us who God resists. James says, "But he gives us more grace. That is why Scripture says: 'God opposes the proud but shows favor to the humble'" (James 4:6). And Peter delivers the same message: "All of you, clothe yourselves with humility toward one another, because, 'God opposes the proud but shows favor to the humble'" (1 Peter 5:5).

Think for a minute about the thorny roadblocks you've encountered throughout your life. Was it humility that led you to those places? I doubt it! In my own experience, humility has never steered me wrong, but pride is an awful GPS. I always end up in a dilemma when I follow pride's directions.

Was it humility that led my friend's daughter Lola into thorns? Nope. Did humility lead me to end my New Year's Eve concert on a sour note? No way! God will resist pride in us because He loves us. If He resists you because of your own pride, don't misunderstand and think that God is rejecting you. It's actually the opposite. He's resisting you so that He can restore you.

Because God is love and He loves perfectly, He lets our paths— as He let Gomer's path—of iddiction get choked by thorns. Hosea 2:7 says, "She will pursue her lovers but not catch them; she will seek them but not find [them]. Then she will think: I will go back to my former husband, for then it was better for me than now" (HCSB).

Often God lets the same thing happen to us. He allows obstacles to trip us up so we will say, "I'll go back to my God and back to my true identity. It was better for me then than it is now." God will let us land in desert places where we feel alone and invisible because He can use that barrenness to bring back our thirst for Him. As Gomer said, "I will go back to my husband, for it was better for me then."

Sister, don't resent God if He resists you. Often what feels like resistance is an affirmation that you belong to God—that He sees you, values you, and loves you way too much to let you go wandering off into iddiction. Sure, it's not as decadent as dark chocolate or as beautiful as a bouquet of roses, but God's way out is better than we could ever imagine when we're tangled in those thorns:

> …the one who loves their children is careful to discipline them.
>
> Proverbs 13:24

Scripture teaches us that a loving parent disciplines her children because of her affection for them. And she resists her children when they are heading down the wrong path. She refuses to let them run wild. Likewise, our loving Father God sometimes needs to stop us in our tracks when our Gomeristic path of iddiction leads us to choices, places, or people that will bring us harm or pain.

You know that promise that "all things work together for good to them that love God, to them who are the called according to his purpose" (Romans 8:28 KJV)? Well, that could mean roadblocks, conflicts, thorns, or walls. These are all things that God can use for our good.

So, Gomer girl, please hear me out on this one. God can use your feelings of invisibility, your insecurity, your identity crisis, and your feelings of inferiority along with all the times you've blown up and blown it. He can use it *all* for your ultimate good!

God can use what hurts us to help heal us.

Really think about where you are right now and what you're struggling with. Ask yourself, *How could this unpleasant feeling—insecurity, rejection, invisibility—actually be good for me? How can God use it to heal me?*

Can bad things truly be good? Can they actually lead you to

something better? Can what feels like resistance from God really be reassuring?

Yes, Gomer girl!

> Sometimes not getting what we want
> gets us where God wants us to be.

Sometimes the dissatisfaction that comes from not getting what we want can actually lead us to a deeply satisfying place—the place where God wants us to be.

So instead of plowing our way through the thorns and crashing into walls, let's pause and consider where we are.

When You Hit a Wall

Let's get back to Gomer's story. Imagine that right now she's paused to acknowledge what she's doing—hanging out with other men—and what she's done—left her husband and children for her old lifestyle. In a moment of quiet, she's looked into her heart to examine where she is and why she's there. For the time being, she's stopped trying to push her way through the tangle of thorns or bang her head against a brick wall. After all, she's trapped and not going anywhere—not anywhere good, anyway.

Imagine Gomer approaching her feelings of invisibility, inse-curity, and discontent not as problems to alleviate but as positions to analyze. Maybe doing this would have helped her to detangle herself from the mess she'd made of her life and turn back home.

As you consider your own situation and think about the times you've been tangled in thorns or stopped by walls, ask yourself some questions:

- Why do I feel insignificant?
- Why am I in constant conflict?
- Why am I angry?
- Why do I act haughty instead of honest?
- Have I received my identity from God, or am I trying to achieve it for myself?
- Why do I feel discontent?
- Am I focused on who God made me, or am I focused on how He should make my circumstances change?
- Why am I so insecure?
- Do I find my sense of self in what I do or in who God made me to be?
- Am I more focused on my way, my wants, and my wisdom—or on God's way, His wants, and His wisdom?

That's quite the list, isn't it? Don't feel pressured to write down responses to every question and feel like you have to solve everything right away. That's impossible! Instead, realize that your feelings and your responses to those questions can serve as fact finders for you.

Did you pick up on that word *fact* in the previous sentence? It's important that you don't just stop with your feelings. Instead, ask God to make your feelings work for you so they can become fact finders you follow to discover truth. That's what my friend's daughter Lola did. The feeling that helped her discover the fact? She was ticked off that her mom made her turn off her phone at 10:00. The truth she came away with? Lola was acting selfish and demanding her own way.

And what about my New Year's Eve debacle? The fact? The audience was tuning me out. The truth? I was insecure and trying to hide that by lashing out. See the difference? God can help make your feelings guides to finding the facts. And finding the facts will lead you to the truth.

Your identity crisis, your sense of insecurity, or your feelings of inferiority are not dead ends. They're simply roadblocks that give you the chance to turn around and find a better path.

But before our paths can change, our hearts and minds must change. How can we do this? We pray truth. In fact, I have a prayer I pray when I find myself in a thorny place and surrounded by the walls my Gomerisms have built. I call this special prayer my Faulty Bow Prayer.

The Faulty Bow Prayer

I call it my Faulty Bow Prayer because it's a quick way to get myself refocused when my iddiction has landed me in a place I don't want to be. If I find myself in conflict with someone else or fighting feelings of insecurity or struggling with the temptation to compare myself with others, I want God to use those situations and feelings as opportunities to turn me around and put me on a better path.

The keyword in this prayer is *turn*. Each letter in the word *turn* represents actions that God will take in our lives to *return* us to Him. The prayer is simple but powerful: *"We turn to You, Lord."* Now, let's get into the heart of the prayer and take a look at what it means to T-U-R-N.

T: *Teach Me Your Ways*

> Teach me Your way, O LORD; I will walk in Your truth…
>
> Psalm 86:11a NASB

When we follow our Gomerisms, we remain familiar with and committed to our own ways. That's why we need to ask God to teach us *His* way. His way never leads us astray. And it never leads us into further selfishness or pride that will only serve to harm us. The reality of being human is that we *will* sometimes find ourselves in those places. But even when we find ourselves there, the more we learn God's way and say, "Not my way but Thy way," the easier the detangling from the thorns or the turnaround from the wall will become.

U: *Unite My Heart with Yours*

> Unite my heart to fear Your name.
>
> Psalm 86:11b NASB

The second half of Psalm 86:11 guides us to ask God to unite our hearts to fear, respect, and highly regard His name and His wisdom. Asking God to grant us purity of heart helps us to honor Him instead of simply lifting up our own ways, our own wants, and our own wisdom.

When you find yourself walled off from where you want to be, don't focus on where you are. Rather, focus on who God is and who He made you to be. Pray: *Focus my heart on You, Lord, so I can honor Your name, not my wayward ways.*

R: Restore the Joy of Your Salvation

> Restore to me the joy of Your salvation and sustain me with a willing spirit.
>
> Psalm 51:12 NASB

This verse is part of Psalm 51, a prayer that King David prayed after he had really blown it and was tangled up in some treacherous thorns. He'd certainly gotten into some kind of trouble! For starters he'd committed adultery. Then he caused even more trouble by having his mistress's husband murdered. When David took a good, honest look at himself, he saw that his heart was more than deeply troubled. He was in agony. He had lost his joy—not his salvation, but his joy. He needed God to create a clean heart in him and restore the joy that originally came with God's salvation.

When you and I find ourselves scratched up by thorns or banged up from hitting the walls too many times, we too need our joy restored. God always restores us to Himself through forgiveness, but we also need to ask Him to reinstall our joy. And He will, my friend! When we shift our focus from "my" to "Thy" and turn back to Him, we will experience His joy because in His presence is "fullness of joy" (Psalm 16:11 NASB).

N: *Never Leave Me or Forsake Me*

> He Himself has said, "I will never desert you, nor will
> I ever forsake you.
>
> Hebrews 13:5 NASB

God has promised He will never leave us or forsake us. So when we pray, *Never leave me*, we aren't asking Him to do something brand-new. We're just affirming our own need for His presence. He never, ever leaves you. Not when you find yourself standing on a stage—insecure, rude, and regretful. Not when you find yourself feeling alone and selfish and tangled in thorns of conflict. He does not, cannot, and will not ever leave you.

As you turn back to Him, you will find Him waiting right there—even in the thorniest place. Besides, Gomer girl, wasn't there once a time when He was tangled in thorns for you—when He hung on a cross and wore those thorns as a crown? He did that to free you from ever having to be tangled in and injured by them ever again, didn't He?

The ultimate reason God lovingly lets us get tangled in thorns is summed up in Romans 8:29: "For those God foreknew he also predestined to be conformed to the image of his Son." God has committed to conform those who belong to Him to the image of His Son. If you belong to Christ, God has a personal commitment to keeping you on His path—even if that means He will allow you to bang into a wall of dissatisfaction or get tangled in thorns of discontent every now and then.

A life spent pursuing self makes us only more insecure. A life lived striving to be seen will just make us feel even more invisible.

A life dedicated to pursuing pleasure doesn't bring happiness. It brings exhaustion.

When you see the result of what God can do in your life, doesn't it make you want to volunteer for an intervention?

Me too, Gomer girl. Me too!

When life
doesn't turn out like I hope,
I won't turn away.
I will turn to God

#TheInvisibleBook

Idolotrinkets

*Now they sin more and more; they
make idols for themselves from their
silver, cleverly fashioned images, all
of them the work of craftsmen.*

HOSEA 13:2

Popcorn was embossed across the creamy white surface of the bowl brimming with fluffy, buttery, fragrant, freshly popped kernels. It was 9:00 p.m. and I stood beside the counter, one hand buried in the popcorn bowl. Next to the popcorn was a bag—not a tiny bag, but a two-pound bag—of dark chocolate M&M's. While one hand mined for the perfect fistful of buttery popcorn, the other rifled through the M&M's bag. As I stood there in my PJ's, shoving popcorn and dark chocolate into my mouth, I had a Gomer moment.

I knew I was a Gomer girl. I was dearly loved, accepted, complete, and—unfortunately—prone to wander. But to be honest, besides my identity crisis that I discovered at my lakeside getaway,

I couldn't put my finger on any other area where I thought I was overly Gomeristic. And then I swallowed a big gulp of reality while standing in my PJ's in the kitchen that night.

I realized I was in a place I didn't want to be—even though it was a completely comfortable, enjoyable place! (I mean, really! Comfort food and PJ's—what could be wrong with that?) But this wasn't about pampering myself. This was about me crossing a line in my relationship with food. I knew something was off, but I just kept ignoring, justifying, and telling myself I would deal with the issue later. Over the years I'd been careful about my health, staying active and watching what I ate. But the older I got, the more nature was doing things to my body that exercise wasn't undoing. I tried to eat less, but I still gained weight!

So at some point—I'm not exactly sure when it was—I just gave up. *Who cares*, I told myself. *I like food!* I began to eat bigger portions. I indulged in those carbs I'd grown tired of limiting. I super-sized French fries—a treat I hadn't eaten in years. And dark chocolate? Well, girl, there aren't enough pages in this book to tell you how much and how often I partook of that all-time favorite! Did I gain weight? Yep. Did I have to buy bigger clothes? Yep. Was I satisfied? Yep. But not for long and not for the right reasons. It didn't take long for my self-image to take a hit, my confidence to become shaky, and my frustration at myself and my lack of self-control to rear its ugly head.

As I stood before my own self-serving feeding trough, I realized how dissatisfied I had become. But the problem wasn't just that I was eating too much. True, I wasn't glad I had gained weight, but that wasn't the sole source of my discontent. I was upset with myself for throwing caution to the wind and reaping the whirlwind of weight gain, a negative body image, and physical fatigue. But not even those undesirables were the main problem. My relationship with food wasn't the problem. It just pointed to the problem.

The problem was my relationship with *me*.

My iddiction had morphed into idolatry.

I had become my own idol, my own god, and food was what I wanted to serve me. In order not to feel invisible, I was finding myself, my security, and my satisfaction in unrestrained eating. I had decided I was going to eat what I wanted and when I wanted it. Like Gomer, I'd made up my mind to go my own way.

I was using food to worship me! I was my own idol, and the food I overindulged in was just a trinket—what I'll call an *idolotrinket*.

When did this happen? How did I get this out of control? Am I willing to get fat just to get what I want?

I couldn't trace when I began to slip out of control. It had been subtle. But isn't that how it always happens? It's hard to detect when something good—like food—begins to become a god thing, but it's easy to see that it all begins with "I."

How I Become My Idol

Becoming your own idol is a slow, subtle process. That's how it began with me and my eating, and I think that's how it happened for Gomer too. Gomer gradually let herself become drawn to other lovers, but they weren't her idols. *She* was her own idol. Her lovers were just the trinkets—the idolotrinkets.

Let's take a moment to sneak into Gomer's thought bubble to figure out what she was thinking. By doing this, we're going to discover how "I" can become your own idol. We're going to spell out idol three different ways, using three different acronyms, to help us understand this thought pattern.

#1: **I d**esire **o**ther **l**overs.

Gomer was caught up in her desire. She wanted more than what she had. Perhaps she thought that what she had wasn't enough or that there had to be something more satisfying out there with someone else. She didn't *phroneo* her heart and her mind on the truth. Instead, her mind wandered away from her true identity as a beloved bride.

Standing in my kitchen with my mouth full of popcorn and M&M's, I saw how I had done the same thing when it came to food. I'd gotten caught up in what I wanted. I'd thought about it, justified it, and ignored a balanced and truthful perspective about it. Instead, when I felt dissatisfied or bored, I ate to be entertained. When I felt mad or sad, I ate to be soothed. And when I felt out of control or stressed out, guess what I did? That's right! I ate to get back in control, to make it seem like I could do what I wanted.

I desired my ultimate "other lover"—*me*. I desired my wants, my wisdom, and my way. I didn't desire weight gain—I desired pleasure. And in my corrupted thinking, I figured I wouldn't feel invisible if I always got what I wanted.

When we become our own idol, it's because of desire—desire gone wrong like a faulty bow.

#2: **I d**on't **o**bey the **L**ord.

Gomer has taught us well that wondering thoughts eventually lead to wandering feet. Her desire for other lovers led to disobedience. She knew she had promised to be faithful to Hosea, but her desire for other lovers was stronger than her desire for the Lord. And so she stepped out.

Long before my salty-and-sweet encounter with a bowl of popcorn and bag of M&M's, I'd had many moments of experiencing a heart full of guilt with a mouth full of food. I felt twinges of conviction telling me I was out of control, but I chose to ignore the Holy Spirit's gentle nudge. I tuned out His whispers that I was made for something more than cramming calories into my mouth in an attempt to satisfy myself. I ignored that still, small voice and, simply put, I disobeyed.

We become our own idol when we start—and then continue— to disobey God. Instead of obeying God's liberating law, we obey the laws of sin and self. And then we find ourselves in a place we never wanted to be.

#3: *I disregard His offer of love.*

Gomer didn't acknowledge that what she had, even after leaving Hosea, was from and because of Hosea. She degraded the love he gave her by offering herself to other lovers. The silver and gold, wool and flax, oil and drink she had was all from Hosea, but she disregarded it by giving it all to another—along with giving credit to another for all the blessings she enjoyed.

I did the same. I'd stopped finding my worth and my satisfaction in God, and so I went to food to find those missing things. Then I gave credit to food for bringing me pleasure, entertainment, and stress relief, which of course led to me desiring even more food.

When we think so little of what we have in God, it's not difficult to degrade and ignore all He has given us. When we regard highly the lust of our eyes, the lust of our flesh, and the pride of

life, we disregard God's love. And this regard comes with a price—
our own degradation.

It's a three-part downward spiral. First, we desire other lovers.
Next, we don't obey the Lord. And finally, we disregard His offer
of love. What do each of these things have in common?

I-D-O-L

The first letter of *idol* is "I." All idolatry is the result of a love of
self—a love of "I."

We become our own idol when we love and serve ourselves
more than we love and serve God. In many ways that's what Gomer
did. She became her own idol. And maybe she did this because
she never fully internalized Hosea's overwhelming love for her. Or
maybe it was because she acted out of her iddiction instead of out of
her identity, and her iddiction led to idolatry—the idolatry of self.

Gomer went for other lovers. But those lovers weren't her idols.
Her lovers were what she used to serve herself, sooth herself, and
satisfy herself. Her lovers were her idolotrinkets.

> Idolotrinkets are good things
> that we turn into god things.

When we feel invisible or insecure, we can use good things—
like food, acceptance, or appearance—as sources of satisfaction

and even self-worship. That's what turns these good things into idolotrinkets.

Food, the approval of others, or shopping aren't wrong, but the importance you attach to them or the way you use them to serve yourself can be wrong. In other words popcorn and M&M's aren't wrong things in and of themselves. I just used them the wrong way!

The root problem for Gomer—and for you and me—is that we are iddicts who have become our own idols using anything we choose—any idolotrinkets that catch our fancy—to satisfy us, please us, or boost our self-worth.

This isn't a new idea. Humans have done this since the beginning of time. Back in Hosea and Gomer's day, Israel's idolotrinket of choice was still that golden calf we first saw at Mount Sinai.

Now, it might seem like a bowl of popcorn and a two-pound bag of M&M's can hardly compare to a golden calf. But we are all calf makers in our own way if we're given the right conditions. That's what we iddicts do—we make idolotrinkets. We take good things and make them god things. We create little golden calves.

Three Steps to Calf Making

Idolotrinkets don't just happen. We create them.

When I was overeating, food didn't just multiply on my plate, grow arms and legs to pry open my mouth, and then crawl inside. No, I chose to hide chocolate, sneak seconds, have a soft drink instead of water, and so on. I created, shaped, and put a lot of effort into making food the idolotrinket that brought me pleasure. I used food to satisfy and serve myself far more than I turned to God to meet my needs. I was far more concerned with serving myself with food than serving God with my choices.

If we identify the steps it takes to make a calf, we can become alert to our daily choices and mindsets and discover how much each of our thoughts and decisions either feeds our iddiction and creates idolotrinkets or confirms our identity.

> Every choice either confirms our
> identity or creates an idol.

Step One: Corrupt Thinking

Do you recall how the Israelites had paused in their pilgrimage out of Egypt and settled at their temporary rest stop at the base of Mount Sinai? Their leader, Moses, had left them for a while, which may have made them feel overlooked and insecure. So they asked his brother, Aaron, to make them a god.

> When the people saw that Moses was so long in coming down from the mountain, they gathered around Aaron and said, "Come, make us gods who will go before us. As for this fellow Moses who brought us up out of Egypt, we don't know what has happened to him."
>
> Exodus 32:1

The Israelites asked Aaron to make them a god. But didn't they already have a god—the one true God? Sure, they did! They weren't thinking straight, though. And apparently neither was Aaron. He made the people a golden calf to worship, and then God told Moses, "Go down, because your people, whom you brought up out of Egypt, have become corrupt" (Exodus 32:7).

The first step in creating an idolotrinket is *corrupt thinking*. Asking Aaron to make a god when they already had one showed some pretty incorrect thinking!

Oh, Gomer girl, when I stalked Facebook that day at the lake, my thinking was a mess. I was a mess! And, as I realized while standing at the kitchen counter with my hand in the popcorn bowl, my obsession with food was not based on correct thinking either. Our Gomer girl didn't use correct thinking when she left Hosea to get what she already had—love and acceptance. She used corrupt thinking.

Step Two: Turning Aside

God told Moses that the people "have turned aside quickly out of the way that I commanded them. They have made for themselves a golden calf and have worshiped it and sacrificed to it and said, 'These are your gods, O Israel, who brought you up out of the land of Egypt!'" (Exodus 32:8 ESV).

Notice that the Israelites didn't totally turn away from God as they watched Aaron make the golden calf at the base of Mount Sinai. They just turned aside. And as they turned aside from God, they turned toward an idolotrinket that they hoped could give them what, in reality, only God could give them.

When we create an idolotrinket, we don't usually create it in direct opposition to God or instead of God. If we did that, we would be choosing to turn away from God. Rather, when we create an idolotrinket, we veer slightly aside and broaden our gaze as we search for something else to satisfy us and give us identity. Instead of being completely satisfied by God and finding our identity in Him, we become satisfied only when we serve ourselves and rely on our idolotrinkets to give us what we need to gain identity.

My friend, idolotrinkets suggest that God isn't enough. We create idolotrinkets in order to complete God. But God is already complete, so all they do is *compete* with God.

> Anything we use to complete God will automatically compete with God.

Step Three: Defying

At the end of Exodus 32:8, God quotes His wayward people. He says they have said, "These are your gods, O Israel, who brought you up out of the land of Egypt!" You wonder how silly the Israelites could have been to give credit to an oversized lucky charm for rescuing them from slavery! Crazy, isn't it? God was the One who rescued them from slavery in Egypt—not a bright, brassy bovine. And yet the people were assigning god qualities to an idolotrinket.

Such an extreme example might seem laughable, but when I shove food into my mouth to soothe and satisfy myself, I'm doing the same thing. I'm assigning god qualities to empty calories— "This is my god who brought me out of my boredom."

When I went on my Facebook frenzy to find acceptance, I was saying, "This is my god that will bring me out of my invisibility."

How about you? Have you ever done the same thing?

Your trendy wardrobe, your perfect children, your fit body, or your illustrious career are not what will "bring you out" of your emotions of insecurity, rejection, or insignificance. They are not what will give you peace and identity. God is the only One who gives us significance. He is the only One who will bring us out of our insecurity and rejection. He is the only One who gives us peace and satisfaction. But when we follow our iddiction and become our own idol, we give our idolotrinkets the credit for what God does.

Our corrupt thinking can cause us to turn aside from God and toward ourselves and our idolotrinkets. And we rely on those idolotrinkets to give us what only God can.

Now, let's dig a little deeper and identify our idolotrinkets.

Idolotrinket Identification

You might already know what idolotrinkets are in your life. You may have just one or two, or you may have an entire charm bracelet full! Or, like me, you might not be sure what exactly has become an idolotrinket in your life. If so, pay close attention to this part!

In order to know who we really are, we've got to get rid of the things that feed our pride or give us a false sense of identity or security. So we need to pause, pray, and ask God to guide us as we discover the six indicators of idolotrinkets.

Indicator #1: Desire

Think for a moment about what you want—what you really, really want. Think about what you want so badly, you can't imagine not having it. It may be something you already have, but you feel a twinge of fear when you imagine losing it.

This might be hard, so think about the things I've listed below and ask yourself, *If I had to choose between faithfulness to Jesus and that person or thing, would I struggle with my choice?*

- People
- Security
- Acceptance
- Identity
- Appearance

Now ask yourself, *Is something that I desire creating an idol to which I'm bound?* If you can't do without it, chances are good that it's an idolotrinket.

Indicator #2: Dwell

Here's a good question to ask yourself: *Do my thoughts create idolotrinkets, or do they confirm my identity in Christ?* What is it that you spend a lot of your time thinking about? What do you tend to dwell on? It's not so much daydreaming about how much you love or want it. It's more that you obsess about how to get it, do it, and have it, or what it would be like if you lost it.

On what do your thoughts most often dwell?

Whatever we think about most is, in effect, serving as our god. If we are always on our minds—*bingo!* Do you see how we can so easily turn into our own idol? And when this happens, our thoughts automatically gravitate toward the people, situations, objects, and feelings that soothe, please, gratify, and affirm us. Those are your idolotrinkets. And where your thoughts dwell—and what they dwell upon—will illuminate your idolotrinkets.

Indicator #3: Defend

If someone questions something that you have, want, or do are you offended? Does that questioning make you feel threatened? Do you feel the need to defend your obsession?

Most of us are guilty of defending, making excuses for, or justifying our actions with thoughts like these: *It's not so bad. It could be worse. Everybody's doing it. I deserve this.*

If you use those kinds of rationalizations, you're probably dealing with an idolotrinket.

Indicator #4: Dedicate

To whom or what are you dedicated? Think about the things you do, the way you think, what seems to be a part of you. Dedication can be a good thing, but it crosses the line when you do anything possible to find a way to make something happen—even if it requires secrecy or sacrifice.

Are you dedicated to doing whatever it takes to keep others from finding out that you are midnight eating or perhaps stashing away cash or maybe hiding what you're reading or watching or...? If you're dabbling in this type of secretive behavior, you're probably dealing with an idolotrinket.

Indicator #5: Deny

It's time to ask yourself, *If other people notice or question me, do I deny what I am doing, thinking about, or wanting?*

If you're afraid that others will find out what you're spending your time, your thoughts, or your money on, that indicates an idolotrinket.

Sweet Gomer girl, we're as sick as our secrets. We won't hide something if we have nothing to hide. But if you're hiding something, it's probably an idolotrinket. I'll be gut-honest. It was this particular "D" that helped me the most in identifying food as an idolotrinket. And now that God has shown me this, with His grace and strength, my view of it—and attachment to it—is being transformed.

Please note, though, that our idolotrinkets often come with habits that take time to break and to replace. If you rely on God and are patient with yourself, they can be overcome.

Indicator #6: Depend

Is there anything you find yourself depending on to make you feel complete or okay with who you are? On what do you depend, and what does that tell you?

If you feel that you need something other than God to complete you, it looks like you've found another idolotrinket.

So what do you think? Did you identify any idolotrinkets? If you have, welcome to my world! Don't be discouraged or down on yourself if you've realized that you have become your own idol and that you're using idolotrinkets to serve the idol of "I." God can redeem anything—including idolotrinkets!

God is teaching me how the formerly powerful idolotrinkets in my life can serve as reminders to look to Him for satisfaction rather than to myself.

I'll show you what I mean.

Serve Self or Honor God

One evening, I sat in a booth at one of those restaurants where they serve you peanuts in a tin trough. "Mama, Don't Let Your Babies Grow Up to Be Cowboys" blared from the speakers, but I could still hear peanut shells crunching beneath people's feet as they walked past us. The restaurant was famous for the steaks it served, but it was famous to me for a different reason—the yeast rolls! These ooey, gooey, buttery yeast rolls simply melted in your mouth. And to make it even better, they came with a side of honey-cinnamon butter to spread on that yummy, baked goodness.

I munched a handful of peanuts while Phil read the menu to me. When our waiter arrived, I ordered steak and a sweet potato. Then I reached my hand into our first basket of yeast rolls, pulled one out, and ate it. As we waited for our dinner, the server appeared with another basket of rolls, and so I ate another one.

When dinner arrived, Phil asked, "Want another roll?" And just as I opened my mouth to say yes, an idolotrinket alarm went off in my head—and in my heart.

Why am I about to say yes? I wondered.

Because I want it, I silently answered myself.

And then the Lord interrupted the conversation I was having with me, myself, and I: "If you have another roll, is that to serve yourself or to honor Me?"

Well, that certainly wasn't a hard question to answer! I wanted another roll to serve the idol of me. I was using that yeast roll right then and there as an idolotrinket. I wanted to eat it because I could, and—if I did eat it—it would serve my senses of entitlement, power, and selfishness. But if I chose to leave that yeast roll in the basket, that choice would honor God. And that innocent roll that I was turning into an idolotrinket would lose its power once I was no longer using it to serve myself. My choice to abstain was a choice to honor God.

Breakthrough! Can I just tell you how grateful I was? Honoring God by saying no to that roll was far more satisfying than stuffing it in my face to serve myself. Finally I was getting it. Using good things to serve me will not make me happy if I'm missing God. Only when the good thing is viewed—and used—as it should be, am I happy. Only when I'm focused on God do I eliminate my idolotrinkets.

Let me state something very clearly: Yeast rolls are not bad things. They are good things. Oh, girl, they are very, very, very good things! Can I get a witness? In fact, I wouldn't be surprised if they'd been served fresh daily in the Garden of Eden! Eating two or even three yeast rolls is not a bad thing. Just because you love and eat lots of yeast rolls doesn't mean you are your own idol and serving yourself. That night for me, though, the yeast rolls had become an idolotrinket because of how I viewed and used them. I was choosing to honor myself with them, not God.

Remember, those objects of your affection like food, acceptance, or appearance are not bad things in and of themselves. But they *can* become idolotrinkets if they're used in the wrong way.

So what do you do when you are confronted with one of your idolotrinkets?

You ask it two questions.

Yes, pretend it is real! Stare it in its imaginary face and ask, "Am I using you to serve myself or to honor God?" And then if it answers, call a therapist. Just kidding! Actually, ask yourself, *Is the way I'm treating this object serving myself or honoring God?*

Gomer girl, I expect you will know the answer. God will show you if you're using that thing, desire, longing, or object to serve yourself or to honor Him. And then ask Him to give you the grace and power to honor Him. He did that for me in the steakhouse with the yeast rolls. It was so clear, and the reward was so immediate.

God honors the woman who honors Him: "for those who honor Me I will honor, and those who despise Me will be lightly esteemed" (1 Samuel 2:30 NASB).

To despise means to consider with disregard. When we use the things God made for us and the desires He gave us to replace Him and serve ourselves, we are considering God Himself with low regard. To take something God made to glorify Himself and remake it into something to serve our own selves is to esteem Him lightly.

We need to place Him above ourselves. Thy wants over my wants. Thy wisdom over my wisdom. Thy way over my way.

Gomer is the poster girl for this, isn't she? She took good things and desires and used them to serve herself instead of to honor God.

So how can we apply this to our own lives? By considering our idolotrinkets and by asking ourselves some honest questions. Think about this with me for a minute.

- If your idolotrinket is approval from others, ask yourself: *Do I desire others' approval to serve my own sense of accomplishment, or do I desire their approval because God will receive honor if others approve of me?*
- If your idolotrinket is popularity, ask yourself: *Am I*

trying to be popular to serve my own sense of significance, or am I seeking popularity because if I am popular, God will be honored?

- If your idolotrinket is acceptance, ask yourself: *Do I long for acceptance to serve my own sense of security, or do I seek acceptance because if I am accepted by others, God will be honored?*

- If your idolotrinket is food, ask yourself: *Am I going for this (cupcake, chocolate, yeast roll, French fry) to serve me, or am I eating it to bring honor to God?*

- If your idolotrinket is appearance, ask yourself: *Am I trying to look (skinny, cute, put-together, sexy) to serve my own sense of identity, or am I dressing like this because my goal is to honor God?*

- If your idolotrinket is your children's good behavior or success, ask yourself: *Am I desiring that my kids behave well and succeed because their good behavior and accomplishments will serve my own ego, or do I desire for them to do their best because it honors God?*

- If your idolotrinket is material things, ask yourself: *Am I using the things I have or the things I want to serve my own needs, or am I using them to honor God?*

- If your idolotrinket is pleasure, ask yourself: *Do I wish for (fancy meals out, sleeping in, traveling, redecorating) to bring me pleasure because it serves me or because, in enjoying these things, God is honored too?*

Oh, girl, the next time it's 9 p.m. and I want a big bowl of buttery popcorn and some dark chocolate M&M's, I'm going to do something before I even put that popcorn bag in the microwave. I'm going to ask myself, *Am I doing this to serve me, or am I doing this to honor God?*

Now, here's the thing, Gomer girl. Some nights God may press on my heart that it's not dishonoring Him to have some popcorn (and, yes, some dark chocolate along with it). The thing is it's about our hearts, not our habits. But our habits reflect our hearts. That's why we need to examine our habits to see our hearts more clearly.

Where our treasure is, there our heart will be also.

That's why we *phroneo* God. That's why we set our affection on Him.

When He is our treasure, our hearts will be drawn toward Him, honoring Him. When we keep our minds on ourselves, though, we become our own treasure and use our idolotrinkets only to enrich ourselves.

I need God to install an idolotrinket alarm in my heart, and I need to check the batteries frequently. Don't you? We need God to keep the mirror of truth ever before us. We need to elevate His wisdom above our own.

There are times when fulfilling your desires *does* honor God. There are times when fulfilling your desires serves yourself but does not honor God. And there are also occasions when you can serve yourself and honor God all at the same time. The condition of your heart is what makes the difference.

What you can be sure of is this:

> God is most glorified in us when we are most satisfied
> in Him.
>
> John Piper

The deep, lasting satisfaction and unshakable identity you long for is exactly what God wants you to have, and it only comes from Him.

You might feel invisible because you're looking for yourself in the eyes of an idolotrinket who cannot see you or give you what you long for. Let's be done with that, okay, Gomer girl? I challenge you to identify and lay down your idolotrinkets because there is only one God—the true God—who satisfies.

> I'm still your GOD, the God who saved you out of Egypt. I'm the only real God you've ever known.
>
> Hosea 13:4 MSG

He's the only God we will ever need.

10

Where Did You Get Your Idolotrinket?

Samaria, throw out your calf-idol! My anger burns against them. How long will they be incapable of purity? They are from Israel! This calf—a metalworker has made it; it is not from God.

<small>HOSEA 8:5-6</small>

"Where'd you get that?" my friend Lori asked as she slid the fuzzy, leopard-print picture into the donation box. The print had a brassy gold frame and the word *Believe* was scrawled across the canvas in a puffy, matted animal-print fabric.

"Someone gave it to me," I said with a laugh.

"Well, it sure doesn't look like something you would choose," Lori remarked.

"Yeah," I said, "and believe it or not, I've had it for almost ten years! I've never really liked it, but because someone gave it to me, I just kept it."

Sighing, I dropped several old frames into the donation box. "What's funny is that the person who gave it to me never comes to my office! So why did I keep something I didn't choose and don't like?"

"We all do it," Lori answered. "Sometimes we don't even realize we're doing it. We just assume that because someone gave it to us, we need to keep it."

And, girl, that is the truth, isn't it?

When I thought about how I'd made room for that leopard print in my office even though I didn't choose, like, or want it, I shook my head. But as I followed my urge to purge that day, I realized that most of what I was donating were things I never chose. Pictures, floral arrangements, jewelry—all these things had been given to me. The people who gave me them thought I would like them, or they wanted me to like them because *they* liked them. And I kept everything because I appreciated their kindness.

In some weird way, I guess I was thinking that *not* keeping what they gave me would dishonor them. Or maybe, not really thinking about it at all, I just took what was given to me and assumed it had to be mine until the day my kids cleaned out my house and moved me into a nursing home! I'm sure that I too have given gifts that the recipients don't like or want. (Friends and family, please note that you have my permission to regift or donate my gifts!)

As I decluttered that day, I kept asking myself, *Why do I still have this? I didn't choose it, I don't like it, and I don't want it.*

My greater concern for us Gomer girls, though, is the stuff in our lives we didn't ask for or want—and these aren't material things like a leopard-print picture or a neon orange scarf.

None of us needs to hold on to things we've been given if they are not things we want in our lives. If we hold on to things we didn't choose or don't want—like incorrect thinking, insecurity, or feelings of insignificance—we begin to live like these things belong to us. And that's the last thing we want!

> Just because we have it
> doesn't mean we chose it.

For instance let's take those idolotrinkets we just learned about. Like an unwanted gift, they might be in our lives because someone else liked them and thought we would too. And so they passed them on to us. Every idolotrinket you go for could be in your little "Idolotrinkets-R-Us" collection because someone else placed it there.

Let me explain a little more. Do you remember what Gomer's dad's name was? (If you don't, it's okay. That was way back at the beginning of this book!) His name was Diblaim, which meant "double portion of raisin cakes" or "double layers of grapecake." Interesting name, isn't it? In Gomer's day, these cakes would be formed after grapes had completely dried. They were then combined with dried apricots, figs, and dates and seasoned with salt and spices. They were thought to possess certain fertility powers—in essence, an ancient aphrodisiac.

Yes, Gomer's dad's name hints that he was totally given up to sensuality.

So we can imagine that little girl Gomer saw and heard much more than she should have and received a very wrong message about what makes a woman attractive. Quite possibly her dad gave her an idolotrinket she didn't need—the acceptance and approval of men. "Gomer," he may have told her, "this is what you need to feel significant."

So Gomer, from a pretty young age, may have received some harmful idolotrinkets. Like I held on to my leopard print in the brass frame, she may have held on to something she never would have chosen on her own.

Since we are trying to see the "me" in Gomer, let's take a little trip a few thousand years into the past. We're going to visit Gomer's city and learn a little more about idolotrinkets. Our sightseeing will help us understand more about the golden calves in our own lives—our idolotrinkets.

Back in Time

Pack your suitcase! We're going on a field trip to the Northern Kingdom of Israel. And watch your step as you get on the bus!

As your tour guide, I'm going to give you a bit of history while we travel. Way back when King Solomon's son Rehoboam came to the throne, he ruled more harshly than his father and grandfather had before him. The Northern tribes (which, for you eager-to-learn tourists, were known as Ephraim) revolted and formed their own government under King Jeroboam around 930 BC.

Now, if you're not a history geek, don't glaze over. This matters to Gomer's story—and to your story—so stay with me. (And there's the promise of snacks at the end of the tour!)

After the Northern tribes revolted, the Northern Kingdom

became known as Israel, and Samaria became the capital city. The Southern Kingdom, known as Judah, kept Jerusalem as its capital. The temple also remained in Jerusalem.

Now look to your left. Rumor has it that the old storefront you see used to be a bar where Gomer hung out before she married Hosea. Some speculate that this was the bar she went back to the first time she walked out on Hosea and her children.

Okay, we'll get off the bus here and walk the rest of the tour. Stay together, and I'll tell you more as we walk.

King Jeroboam was worried about keeping his new kingdom cohesive, especially when his people were still so attached to their customs of worship and sacrifice at the temple in Jerusalem. (You can read more about this in 1 Kings 12:25-31.) To sum up the situation, King Jeroboam was afraid his kingdom would revert to the House of David (in Judah) if the people kept going to the temple to make sacrifices. So the king made two golden calves and said to the Israelites, "You have gone to Jerusalem long enough. Here are your gods that brought you up from Egypt."

Let's pause here. Looking to your right, you can see the crumbled remains of one of the shrines Jeroboam set up. And you may be wondering, *Why a calf?*

Good question! The calf and the bull had important roles in the art and the religious texts of the ancient Near East. Some Jewish scholars surmise that Jeroboam's golden calves were to correspond to the cherubim of Solomon's temple. They were to be seats or pedestals upon which the invisible god would stand. Many also think that the golden calves were associated with the storm god Baal. Gomer and her fellow Israelites were called "calf kissers," and it's also recorded that they were Baal worshippers.

In any case Jeroboam's calf construction wasn't an odd or foreign concept to Israel, so it was probably no big deal for the people to pucker up and kiss the calves! And by the time Gomer and Hosea lived here—about 200 years later—Israel was heavy into idol worship.

Walk with me a few more steps, and we'll end our tour here. As you look around, you can see that this is the general area where the Israelites were expected to worship. Here in what was once called the Northern Kingdom, festivals and sacrifices were ordained for the new religious centers with one calf at Bethel and the other at Dan.

Now, as we end our tour, please gather your belongings and be sure to fill out this survey to let us know how you enjoyed the tour. And about those snacks I promised earlier? I hear that Yoshi's Cafe has scrumptious goose skin cracklings with fried onions and matzah balls. Enjoy, and thanks very much for coming!

Gifts We Never Wanted

That was fun, wasn't it? I took you on this goofy, geeky excursion not only for the history clarification but also to bring some understanding to your own history. Thinking about the Israelites may help you figure out why you go for the idolotrinkets you go for when you're yearning to find acceptance or identity.

Sometimes we aren't the ones who erect the idolotrinkets we run to. Sometimes someone who has great influence over us erects them. As Jeroboam told the people of Israel, "Here are your gods."

So think about it with me. Is there anything in your life that you're drawn to—something you find yourself going for, something you feel has power over you—that someone else set up and told you in so many words, "Here, this is your god"?

The way in which Gomer's father lived—and the man he was—could very well have set up a god of promiscuity and told Gomer, "Here, this is your god." It wasn't a billboard announcement. It was actually more effective than that. Suppose Gomer only received attention from her father when she looked a certain way. That was her father's way of saying, "Here, this is your god." Suppose she picked up on the fact that he only valued women who were sexy or available. That was his way of setting up a golden calf for Gomer and telling her, "If you want to be somebody, you need to show off your body. This is your god."

Do those examples help you to understand how your own idolotrinkets may have been placed in your life by someone else?

Maybe you had a parent who set up an idolotrinket of sorts—a mindset, an object, a standard—and, without words, that parent told you by example, "This is your god." Or it could be that our culture handed you an unwanted idolotrinket along with the message, "Here, this is your god." You find yourself drawn to that mini-god—the idolotrinket—without even knowing why it's so attractive to you. It could be anything—money, appearance, acceptance, significance. It could even be moral goodness or education. Oh, idolotrinkets come in endless shapes and sizes!

Did you know that anyone who has influence in our lives has the potential to gift us with an idolotrinket? And without even realizing it, we can accept it, adopt it into our lives, and go for it whenever we feel lacking in satisfaction and identity. Without even realizing it, we can embrace this idolotrinket to ease our insecurity and make us feel less invisible. All of this can happen despite the fact that, had we realized what we were accepting, we never would have chosen that mini-god.

So how do we allow these idolotrinkets to sneak into our lives, and what can we do to keep them from entering in the first place?

We're going to take a look at five different idolotrinkets that we Gomer girls commonly have in our lives. The list isn't limited to five, but these are pretty popular in our culture, so see if any ring true for you.

Perfect Performance

Perfect performance could be an idolotrinket that a parent erected for you back when you were a child. Or perhaps a boss, spouse, or influential teacher or coach has given you the message that you're only as good as your performance. If you fail, you are a failure. If you try harder, you'll be applauded. If you do your best, though, and someone else is still better than you, you're back to square one.

Perfect performance is an idolotrinket we go to when we want to satisfy our need for approval, but it's always a losing battle. That particular idolotrinket can never, ever be satisfied. We'll never be perfect!

It's important to remember that the person who set up that idolotrinket for you most likely had your best interest at heart. They meant well, and they didn't intend for you to feel like a constant failure. They gave you the idolotrinket because they truly thought they were giving you what was best for you. But just because they thought it was a gift to push you to be more than your best doesn't mean that the gift was good for you. It's an idolotrinket you could spend your life sprinting after but never catch.

If you currently have the idolotrinket of perfect performance in your life, do you want to keep it? Is it something you would have chosen for yourself? Would you give it to someone you love? There's a difference between encouraging the people we love to do their best and pushing them to be the best. So please be wise, my friend. If you had a parent who gave you that particular idolotrinket, there's a good chance you're handing it down to your children without even realizing it. Oh, Gomer girl, don't give them something you wouldn't have chosen!

Perfect performance isn't where it's at—ever. When you need to feel accepted and approved, sister, don't run to an idolotrinket to meet your needs. Run to Jesus. He has accepted you. You are good enough because He is good. And He is enough.

Perfect Appearance

Having a perfect appearance is an idolotrinket that our culture—courtesy of the media, advertising, and the advent of photo-editing software—has set up for us. The results of that gift? Feeling the need to please the mini-god of perfection every time you look in the mirror. Talk about a struggle!

If this is your idolotrinket, you've probably received it little by little over the years—from photoshopped magazine pictures featuring skinny, flawless, perfectly put-together celebrities to the fabulously filtered Instagram images on your phone. Every picture of perfection you see makes that idolotrinket grow and makes you feel like you'll never measure up.

You might choose to spend your time and money on products and procedures that get you closer to your goal of perfection, but you'll never achieve it. That's because what you're trying to achieve—the perfection you see in the photos—doesn't exist in reality. The idolotrinket of perfect appearance is a big, fat lie!

> We can let go of our need for perfection
> and embrace God's perfection.

The substance of this particular idolotrinket is hidden insecurity, and it shows up in real women—women who are beautiful just the way they are—striving to be something other than their true selves. In fact, the driving force behind women striving for perfect appearance is the desire to be loved, accepted, and complete. And, Gomer girl, we're *already* loved, accepted, and complete in our imperfection. God loves us just the way we are, and all we need to do is look into the mirror of His Word to see and experience this. We can let go of our need for perfection and embrace His perfection. Isn't that a relief?

Perfect Kids

If you're a mom, this idolotrinket might hit close to home. When you have your idolotrinkets—your perfect children—lined up with such bright and shiny faces, it certainly makes you feel like a success. Your kids look perfect, so you must be perfect too! And this idolotrinket rules on the throne of comparisons. It's easy to compare children's behavior, grades, musical or athletic abilities, appearance—you name it!

This peer-driven idolotrinket is a shaky one because it's only as good as your kids' next performance. But then one day, a child blows it. He fails a class. She steals candy from the grocery store. He refuses to go to church. She cheats on a test. He falls in with a bad crowd of friends. Suddenly the idolotrinket is shattered—and you're clearly the one who blew it. You didn't try hard enough as a mom. You're not good enough—and you never were.

It's yet another losing battle. No matter how great your children's behavior is or how many awards they bring home, someone else's kids will always be better behaved or more successful. But you are not your children's successes or failures. Your identity is in Christ. So you are allowed to do your best as a parent and tell yourself, *It's good enough.* Love your children and then let go of perfection and hand everything else over to God. After all, He loves all of you more than enough, and His love is perfect.

Perfect Home

Here's another peer-driven idolotrinket—the perfect home. When we're caught up in comparisons, we can easily become enslaved by this idolotrinket. It's one we commonly run to when we're desperately seeking popularity, identity, or approval. It's bad enough when we visit a friend who has just remodeled or redecorated and we compliment her style while pangs of envy rage inside us. And we only make it worse when we come home, fire up our computer or smart phone, and head over to Pinterest where we see a cozier couch, better wall hangings, or more creative centerpieces. Suddenly that idolotrinket we ran to for affirmation is once again impossible to obtain.

Striving for the perfect home—or the perfect anything, really—is our way of saying, "See me! Like me! Want me! Choose me!" Yet no matter how lovely your home is, you'll always discover someone else's is even lovelier. Yep, it's that same old thing that happens when we chase after the idolotrinket of perfection.

Here's something reassuring: We are not identified by the quality or beauty of our homes. We are more than our decorating skills. Our value is not attached to what we own. And we are not how we *feel* about our homes. Our homes are not to be used as sources of approval or identity. Our homes are to be enjoyed—imperfections and all. Because God welcomes us into His heart, we can welcome others into our homes. So go ahead and be who you are and live who you are—loved, accepted, and complete in Christ.

Perfect Husband

Whether we're single or married, a perfect husband is the next idolotrinket that's easy to gravitate toward. Single gals have it tough because we live in a culture that declares if we're not married, we're not whole. And if you are married—well, that guy had better be as fabulous as the heroes of romance novels or the men on the silver screen!

And so we set out on the quest to find—or create—the ideal idolotrinket husband who will satisfy us and give us the identity we long for. But what if he isn't handsome? What if he snaps at the kids? What if he isn't a strong spiritual leader? What if he doesn't bring you roses or close the toilet seat or wash the dishes or take the dog out or bring home a six-figure income?

What if he isn't perfect?

The image of a perfect husband can't be our idolotrinket. It's impossible to find our identity and ultimate security in a man. You are complete in Christ, Gomer girl. If you are married, your husband does not complete you—he complements you. Only God can complete you. If you are single, you are not incomplete. You are complete in Christ.

I'm guessing that one or more of those five idolotrinkets may be sitting on a shelf in your heart. If so, it's wise to spend some time in prayer and reflection, remembering that others may have placed that idolotrinket there a long time ago. It may take a while to stop running after it, but you'll get there.

I bet you're intuitive enough to have my idolotrinket pegged by now. Perfect performance! I'm not exactly sure where it came from, but I do know that I grabbed it fast and made it my own.

In fact, I can look all the way back to a certain first-grade field trip that points to my need for perfect performance. I don't remember where we were going, but I do remember what happened as we were walking to our destination. We were walking along a gravel road in Georgia—and it was uphill. Wanting so much to please my teacher, I asked if I could help carry her camera. She handed over the camera and told me to be careful with it, which I was—until I slipped on a particularly grumpy piece of gravel and fell flat on my first-grade face! My knees began to burn and bleed, and I started crying, "Sorry! Sorry!"

I can still see the image of my teacher picking up the pieces of the broken camera. And while I can't remember the exact words she spoke to me, I do recall that she looked at me with a scowl and said something to the effect of, "Don't ask me to carry my camera if you're going to drop it and break it." And then I remember her silence that followed.

I don't remember if my first-grade teacher had any concern for my scraped knees or my wounded spirit. All that stays with me is the scolding followed by her icy silence. I was a little girl who clung to an idolotrinket of acceptance, and my teacher added to that idolotrinket. It was as if she'd said, "Here is your god, Jennifer. If you want to be accepted, you need to perform perfectly. But if you blow it, you will be shunned and shamed."

Now, believe me, I know that children are very capable of misinterpreting actions and words and assigning incorrect meanings to events. But either way, this event sticks in my memory because it contributed to the making of my idolotrinket—even if it was my misinterpretation that added strength to the construction of my little idol.

You may be a woman reading this right now and completely understanding it. You've been that girl—you currently own an idolotrinket of acceptance that was created many years ago. If so, can you trace where that idolotrinket came from? Can you recall who created it? And can you think of how you've helped build and strengthen it over the years? By examining the origins of our idolotrinkets, we can determine if we really chose them—and if we want to keep them.

Do you get peace and delight from your idolotrinket?

Does it really give you the acceptance you are longing for?

Do you find your identity in it?

I doubt it. In fact, I know the answer is no—or eventually will be no—to all of the above questions.

The Illusion and Delusion of Idolotrinkets

We'll never be satisfied by idolotrinkets, and the prophet Jeremiah helps us understand why. In Jeremiah 10:1-2, he gives us this wise warning:

> Hear what the Lord says to you, people of Israel. This
> is what the Lord says: "Do not learn the ways of the
> nations or be terrified by signs in the heavens, though
> the nations are terrified by them."

Jeremiah warned Judah—and us—not to learn or follow the ways of the nations. Just because something is the cultural norm or your family norm or even has been your personal norm doesn't mean that you need to follow along. Sometimes the ways of the nation or the ways of others may not seem evil or bad. In Jeremiah 10:3 (NASB), the prophet describes the customs of the people as delusional. It's interesting that the ways of the nation are not necessarily despicable, disappointing, or disgusting, isn't it? If they were, we probably wouldn't be as apt to get sucked in.

Delusional. Misguided. Confused. These are all words Jeremiah uses to describe the people who establish and follow the ways of the nation. Have some idolotrinkets been erected for you because others have been misguided or delusional?

The five idolotrinkets we explored earlier—perfect performance, perfect appearance, perfect kids, perfect home, and perfect husband—are delusional in that they set up the lie that these things are ultimate, attainable, and worthy of your pursuit. Along with these idolotrinkets comes the false promise that the attainment of these things will give you your identity while making you feel accepted, secure, and satisfied. That's a lot to promise!

But please remember this: *They are empty lies.* In fact, Jeremiah calls them "a scarecrow in a cucumber field."

> Like a scarecrow in a cucumber field, their idols cannot speak; they must be carried because they cannot

walk. Do not fear them; they can do no harm nor can
they do any good.

Jeremiah 10:5

Who would worship a scarecrow in a cucumber field?

Uh...me? I have. I did. I do. I do it when my own faulty wisdom
says, "I need more Facebook followers in order to have identity."
Or when I adopt corrupt thinking and tell myself, "I must perform perfectly to be acceptable." Or when I act out of my iddiction
and run to food for stress relief, I am worshipping a scarecrow in
a cucumber field. Anyone who would do that is delusional, right?

Oh, Gomer girl, that is the point! Whoever set up those idolotrinkets and told you they were your gods planted a scarecrow in
the cucumber field of your life and called it sacred. But those idolotrinkets are empty—and even laughable. What's more, they hold
absolutely no power.

Seriously, think about that! The only power an idolotrinket
has is the power you give it. The number of Facebook followers I
have has no power over me unless I give that number the power to
impact me. The approval we have—or don't have—from others
has no power unless we let it.

A lie can only have power over you if you believe it.

A lie can only have authority in your life if you accept it.

Jeremiah reinforces this at the end of verse 5 by telling us those
empty idolotrinkets that others erected for us cannot speak and
cannot walk—they have to be carried and we have to speak for
them. So if they can't speak, why do we listen to them? And if
they can't walk, why do we try to follow them? If they have to be

carried—from one year to the next, from one generation to the next—why in the world are we doing the heavy lifting? And if we have to speak for them, why are we even bothering to put words in their mouths?

Are you lugging around a heavy golden calf? Are you putting words in its mouth? And if you are, is this idolotrinket one you chose to carry and speak for?

Even if you unwittingly adopted an idolotrinket from someone you love, that doesn't mean that your loved one is awful or mean. They probably adopted the same idolotrinket because of their own need. They—like Israel, Gomer, you, and me—hadn't identified with their true identity either. They didn't realize they were the beloved, so they grabbed an idolotrinket that would make them be happy, be better, or be somebody.

Ultimately, though, any time we gravitate toward an idol-otrinket, it's because we are—as Jeremiah wrote—delusional. We are delusional enough to be our own idol. We have diluted thinking—corrupt thinking. But let's try something new. As we keep on this journey together, let's start to replace the image of our idol-otrinket with the image of a worn-out scarecrow in a cucumber field. It sounds silly, but it will help us begin to adopt correct thinking about what an idolotrinket really is.

Redeem Through Prayer

If it's not easy to see your idolotrinket as a scarecrow in a cucumber field, I understand! That is kind of odd, I know. But there's something else you can do when an idolotrinket starts calling your name. You can break its power through prayer! And as you pray,

God will redeem that idolotrinket. That's because idolotrinkets are usually good things that we—or someone else—turned into little god things. But they can be redeemed and returned to their intended purpose.

When I tell you how I organize my prayer to break an idolotrinket's power in my life, you're going to laugh. Here's the word I use: I-D-O-L. Seriously! But the purpose of the *idol* prayer is to get rid of the idols in my life and let God redeem them to use for His glory. So let's take a look!

I: Incline My Heart

> Incline my heart to your testimonies, and not to selfish gain!
>
> Psalm 119:36 ESV

Sister, when we ask God to tilt us toward Him, He always will. I'm naturally inclined to selfishness. I want what I want when I want it! But God already has—and will continue to—incline my heart toward Him. When I feel a flutter of insecurity and am tempted to soothe it with an idolotrinket, I ask God to draw me toward Him and away from that thing I'm trying to use to replace Him. And God, who redeems everything—including our wayward impulses—draws me away from that idolotrinket and toward His presence. So when you think you hear the voice of an idolotrinket speaking your name, speak the name of the Lord and ask Him to incline your heart toward Him.

D: Delight in God

> Delight yourself in the Lord, and he will give you the
> desires of your heart.
>
> Psalm 37:4 ESV

When I am drawn to one of my idolotrinkets with its shiny promises, I continue with my idol-busting prayer. I pray, *I delight in You, Lord. This thing—this idolotrinket—may be delightful but it is not my source of delight. You are! So put in me the desire I need to have right now. Make my desire for honoring You stronger than my desire for serving me.*

And, girl, He does! As you incline your heart toward Him, you begin to delight in Him. He answers your prayer at the very same time you are praying it. Oh, what an amazing Father!

O: Open My Eyes

> I pray that the eyes of your heart may be enlightened,
> so that you will know what is the hope of His calling,
> what are the riches of the glory of His inheritance in
> the saints, and what is the surpassing greatness of His
> power toward us who believe.
>
> Ephesians 1:18-19 NASB

We often make a beeline toward an idolotrinket when we feel hopeless or in need of a boost. If you find that happening to you, ask God to open your eyes so you can see the hope to which you are called. An empty idolotrinket will never give you hope, and often you need to have your spiritual eyes opened so you can see that truth clearly. A scarecrow in a cucumber field doesn't give you much hope when you're feeling down, does it? So keep that in mind as you pray and ask God to open your eyes.

L: Love the Lord

> Love the LORD your God with all your heart and with all your soul and with all your strength.
>
> Deuteronomy 6:5

The final phase of your idolotrinket-redeeming prayer is telling God you love Him. And tell Him you love Him, not just with your words but also with your whole heart, life, strength, and soul. As you express your love for God with every part of who you are, your desire for that idolotrinket will start to shrink. And even if it doesn't disappear right away, your love for God will grow and help you to continue to incline your heart toward Him.

Oh, Gomer girl, those idolotrinkets are not all they're cracked up to be!

By the end of the book of Hosea, Israel had figured that out. The Israelites were worn out from their waywardness. They finally realized how futile and damaging their idolatry had been. They had discovered that depending on anything and anyone other than the one true God was doing them no good at all. In the next chapter, we'll see how Gomer came to the same conclusion about her lovers.

We need to give up our idolotrinkets not only because they will never satisfy us but also because they will eventually enslave us.

> The idolatry of self leads to
> the slavery of sin.

So let's begin the process of stripping those idolotrinkets of their power and redeeming them through prayer. Here are the words to write on the tombstone you'll erect when you bury your idolotrinkets once and for all:

> We will never again say "Our gods" to what our own hands have made, for in you the fatherless find compassion.
>
> Hosea 14:3

"The
ways of the Lord
are right;
the righteous
walk in them."

Hosea 14:9b

11

The Slave Block

*They sow the wind and reap the
whirlwind...Israel is swallowed up; now
she is among the nations like something
no one wants. For they have gone up
to Assyria like a wild donkey wandering
alone. Ephraim has sold herself to lovers.*

HOSEA 8:7-9

It may have begun way back in 2003 with the social network Myspace. Or maybe it happened because every time we switch on our computer screens, we see words on the desktop like "my" documents, "my" music, and "my" downloads. I'm pretty sure that iPhones, iPads, iPods, and iMacs reinforced it. (Notice what letter each of these products starts with?) Yes, we are a generation obsessed with me, myself, and I! In fact the Oxford Dictionaries International Word of the Year 2013 was *selfie*!

Me, myself, and I—ay yai yai!

There's a reason *idol* begins with "I"! When it's always about my way, my wants, and my will, those Gomerisms lead us smack-dab into iddiction—and our iddiction leads to idolatry. And from there it only gets worse.

Remember how our girl Gomer said, "I *desire* other lovers. I *disobey* our Lord. And I *disregard* His offer of love"? Gomer didn't *phroneo* truth; she desired other lovers. She followed her way, her wants, and her will and disobeyed the Lord. She became an iddict who disregarded both God's and Hosea's offers of love, and that disregard led to despair. Gomer probably didn't realize this was the path she was headed down, but the cost of other lovers can be steep. Her iddiction led her to idolatry, and her idolatry led her to slavery. What she considered a choice ended up putting her in chains.

Let's check back in with our Gomer girl and see where she's been and where she's going to end up.

Rumors have been growing in Israel. It seems like everyone knows about Gomer. Hosea heard she'd been going from man to man. But lately Gomer hasn't been seen out at the high-end places in town. And remember your chatty friend from chapter eight, the one who called you on her cell phone? Well, she just called to inform you that someone recently spotted Gomer in the run-down section of town—that place near the homeless shelter. It seems as if Gomer's party days have come to an end.

Like a tattered newspaper on a train, Gomer has been passed around so much that she's no longer wanted. The men who have been falling over each other to have her no longer turn their heads when she walks through the door of the bar. Their gifts—the extra cash, the cute nighties, the special spa days—aren't arriving any-more. And there's a reason for this—the guys have grown tired of

Gomer. Everyone has had her, and there's nothing left in the conquest. She was enjoyed for a time, but the novelty is gone.

Once showered with diamonds, Gomer has now been stripped of her dignity. She was exciting to each new lover—until a younger, more promising woman took her place. Pursued and then discarded time and time again, Gomer has grown weathered and worn. And as her allure and attractiveness have faded, Gomer has grown desperate. Those lovers who gave her all she was longing for—the men who fed and clothed her, wined and dined her—are no more. Gomer has gone from the latest headlines to yesterday's news. She's journeyed from Chanel to chains, from Prada to prostitution.

Hosea's once-beloved bride has become overlooked. Desperate, destitute, and discarded, her only option now is full-time, whatever-it-takes prostitution. These days she has to pay for her own bread and water, wool and flax, and oil and drink.

The Slave Block

Gomer has fallen about as low as she could go. And this is where she's landed—standing on a slave block, waiting to be sold. Just one of several slaves being auctioned off to the highest bidder at the local slave market, Gomer must have one thought running through her mind: *How did I get here?*

Smarter brains than mine who have studied the book of Hosea think that Gomer could have wound up on the slave block because she thought that was her only choice. She had to sell herself in order to meet her basic needs—food, shelter, clothing. Others surmise that after leaving Hosea, Gomer may have lived with a man and became his wife in a common-law marriage sort of way.

Because she was this man's property, he had the right to put her up for sale (after he'd grown tired of her, of course). Yet other scholars believe that Gomer could have become a prostitute and the pimp who had employed her was looking to get as much out of her—and for her—as possible. Also during this period in Israel, many women were actually temple prostitutes—either by choice or out of necessity—and that could have been Gomer's situation.

We don't exactly know how Gomer wound up on that slave block, but we do know that she was no longer free. The party had ended. She had gone from glorious to disgraced. As God said of Israel, Gomer "became as vile as the thing [she] loved" (Hosea 9:10).

Gomer's choices led to her chains.

When we leave God for other lovers of self or sin, we pay a huge price. Unrestrained desire always goes wrong and gives us despair instead of the delight we were aiming for. Like Gomer, we find ourselves stuck in a place we don't want to be and ashamed of what brought us there.

Listen to Hosea's description of the nation of Israel. Does this sound like where Gomer ended up? Does this sound like us when we find our faulty choices have landed us stuck in sin?

> Israel is swallowed up; now she is among the nations
> like something no one wants. For they have gone up to
> Assyria like a wild donkey wandering alone. Ephraim
> has sold herself to lovers.

> Hosea 8:8-9

Israel had turned to superpowers like Assyria and Egypt instead of turning to God for national security and identity. It sure sounds like what Gomer did and what we do, doesn't it? Swallowed up. Wandering alone. Feeling like something no one wanted. That's what happens when we go to our idolotrinkets for security. Feeling desperate and stuck, we think we'll always be chained to invisibility and left with an unquenchable thirst for identity.

God knows that none of us want to be stuck in chains, that we never planned to become enslaved by the very things we once thought we wanted. But it happens. What starts as a small choice and a step in the wrong direction becomes a chain that binds us to defeat.

Let me give you an example of how this works. When a woman's idolotrinket is acceptance—the "please, please like me" syndrome—her slave master will be insecurity because she's governed by the fear of not performing well. And she will never know if she has done enough to please that fake god. She'll never know if she's good enough.

What about a woman whose idolotrinket is significance—the "please validate and esteem me" syndrome? Her slave master will be an identity crisis because she'll always be imprisoned by the constant striving to be somebody, to matter, to earn affection and identity. She'll never be able to rest in who she is because she doesn't even know who she is. And because there will always be someone more significant than her, she'll constantly wonder, *Who am I?*

And then there's the idolotrinket of pleasure or comfort— the "please satisfy me" syndrome. That woman's slave master will be discontentment because she'll always need and want more— and there always *will* be more to need and want! As much as she obtains, she'll never be content. Someone else will always have something more or something better. She's owned by the nagging thought that there really is more and better for her if only she could just find it.

Do you recognize any of these idolotrinkets? Have any of your choices become your chains? Do you recall my idolotrinket? When I choose to seek acceptance from perfect performance, I am chained to something unattainable that chokes me. And I need something to set me free.

Women Caught in the Act of Being Human

Gomer was not the only woman enslaved by her sins and caught in the web of her own choices. We've all felt swallowed up by invisibility, and we've all wandered alone in insignificance. We've all felt stuck in the muck and uck of our bad choices that have morphed into chains. You may have done something in your life that you feel so guilty about that you struggle to accept God's forgiveness as well as accept the *you* He accepts. Maybe you can't imagine God looking upon you with love ever again. Or perhaps you're enslaved in a lie that says you're only as good as your latest performance. So when you blow it, you beat yourself up.

We all have those Gomer moments when we feel like the chains will never come off. Sometimes we've arrived at that point by way of sinful choices or a heart that strayed from Him. At other times we can't point to any actions that got us wrapped in chains. We've simply found ourselves living out our humanity, struggling with weaknesses, and fighting off lies.

And not only can we feel trapped in sin or weakness—we can also feel stuck in the very shame that sin or weakness creates. What's more, that shame can be just as choking as the sin itself because of what shame does to us.

Shame Isolates

Jesus once met a woman who had been caught in a Gomer moment. Jesus was teaching in the temple when some scribes and Pharisees brought this woman who had been caught in adultery to Him and "set her in the center of the court" (John 8:3 NASB). She'd evidently been yanked out of bed and dragged to where the Israelite men were listening to Jesus teach. Imagine the shame she felt as she stood before Him and the other religious leaders of the day. It would be like bringing someone into the foyer of your church and encouraging everyone to stop and stare.

Gomer too must have felt utter shame as she was set in the center of the slave auction with all eyes upon her. Everyone most likely knew who she was and where she had come from. As a woman clearly removed from proper society, she had to have felt the sting of separation as she stood on that platform. The sting of isolation had to shoot through her wounded soul as tears coursed down her cheeks. The shame of this experience must have set her to wondering why she'd traded in the security and identity she had as a beloved bride for the humiliation and shame of this moment. Was she the only one who'd ever been so stupid, so selfish, and so stuck?

When we are caught in sin or selfishness, we too can feel like we're the only one in that predicament. But sometimes we're caught there because we're simply being human. We're always going to stumble and make mistakes—and this makes us feel ashamed, like we shouldn't be that weak or incapable. I know, Gomer girl. It makes no sense, but it's still so real.

I recall one night when I was a college student and needed someone to walk me from the student center back to my dorm. Even though I use a white cane to help me navigate my blindness, I do a lot better when I can also hold on to someone's arm. But back in my college days, I didn't carry my cane everywhere.

On this particular night, none of my usual friends were around, and I was starting to stress out. *Who will walk me to my dorm?* I wondered. *I don't think I can get there alone.* While I was trying to push back my inner panic, another student approached me to ask me a question. *Thank You, God!* I whispered to myself.

I didn't know Chelsie well, but I knew her well enough to swallow my pride and ask her to walk me back to my dorm. Now, please know that I was a ton more uncomfortable with my blindness back then. I was painfully self-aware, and all I wanted was to be normal and to fit in. I never wanted to be needy. So asking Chelsie to walk with me was a pretty big deal.

Because I didn't have my cane with me that night, I was totally dependent upon Chelsie's prompts to step up or down and whatever else would keep me from falling on my face. Chelsie, though, had no experience helping a blind person navigate her way—and so as not to burden her, I didn't bother to explain how best to help me (#notsmart). You can imagine how well this went!

As we walked I held Chelsie's elbow and tried to pay close attention to where we were while counting my steps to the curb. I thought I knew the campus pretty well, but I was wrong. When I got to the first curb, I stepped—sort of! I staggered and stepped down really hard.

"Oh!" Chelsie exclaimed.

"It's okay," I reassured her before promptly jamming my toe into the next curb.

"Oh!" Chelsie said again.

"It's okay," I replied.

This pattern continued for a while until I stumbled going from street to sidewalk. But this time instead of Chelsie saying oh and me saying that it's okay, I blurted out, "I'm sorry!"

I'm sorry? I wondered. *Why did I say that?* And then Chelsie responded in a chipper tone, "It's okay!" Talk about a dysfunctional moment!

I still think about this exchange with Chelsie. Why did I feel the need to apologize? I felt ashamed that I couldn't figure out the steps on my own, but in reality there was absolutely no reasonable, logical basis for me to say I'm sorry. But I was a woman caught in the very act of being human. I felt shame—unfounded shame, but shame nevertheless. I was a young college student who was blind, for heaven's sake! And sweet Chelsie was a college freshman who didn't know how to handle the situation. Nobody had done anything wrong. We were simply two young women living out our less-than-perfect humanity. And because of this, I felt the need to pick up a big rock of condemnation and throw it at myself.

You may identify with my college story for altogether different reasons, but we'll always have one thing in common—feeling shame for being caught in the act of being human. We feel like this every time we blow it, even if we're not intentionally choosing to sin. We make mistakes. We forget things. We let friends down. We can't keep up with our housework. We're impatient with our husband or our children. And when we're caught in the act of being human, we forget our identity as a loved, complete, and accepted woman—and we start to scramble for identity.

Shame isolates you while whispering lies into your ear: *You're the only woman who can't pull off life. Everyone else is perfect. You're the only one who is a wreck. Nobody else struggles with that.* Shame catches you at your weakest, most vulnerable moment, shakes its accusing finger at you, and says, "Ah-hah! Caught you, you saggy-kneed human!"

When we're caught in the act of being human, we allow shame to grab the spotlight and illuminate our low self-esteem, perfectionism, or excessive guilt. And our instinct is to hide—to isolate ourselves—because we're certain we're all alone in this mess.

Oh, Gomer girl, don't hide! You're not the only one. *Everyone* sins. *Everyone* stumbles. *Everyone* blows it. *Everyone* struggles.

But *everyone* is also loved—and accepted. So don't let shame lie to you and tell you that you must hide. You might be stuck right now in a place you don't want to be, but God doesn't identify you based on where you are. He identifies you based on *who* you are and *whose* you are. You are His. If you feel the need to hide, run to Him and hide in Him. There you'll feel the covering of His love rather than the exposure brought by shame.

Shame Exposes

Shame does more than isolate. It can expose us, leaving us feeling unprotected and vulnerable. That's what happened to the poor woman who stood in front of Jesus. In John 8:4, the Pharisees said to Jesus, "Teacher, this woman has been caught in adultery, in the very act" (NASB).

Now, it doesn't take much imagination to know what a woman caught "in the very act" of adultery was—or was not—wearing. Believe me, this woman was exposed! Gomer was probably exposed too as she stood on that slave block. She was there so purchasers could assess her, so it was likely she wasn't clothed in the way she would have preferred.

The woman caught in adultery couldn't cover herself, Gomer

couldn't cover herself, and when we're caught sinning—or even just caught in the act of being human—we can't cover ourselves either. We feel just plain exposed, which is what shame does to us. In fact, the word *shame* comes from a word meaning "to cover."

Of course, the settings that Gomer and the woman in the temple found themselves in were not your typical settings for wearing your birthday suit! But it isn't being naked that should make anyone feel shame. It's the awareness of that nakedness and exposure that makes us feel shame.

Think about the dress code for the Garden of Eden—birthday suits for everyone! Genesis 2:25 says, "Adam and his wife were both naked, and they felt no shame."

But after Eve took a big bite out of her innocence, she suddenly wanted to change the dress code! "Then the eyes of both of them were opened, and they realized they were naked; so they sewed fig leaves together and made coverings for themselves" (Genesis 3:7).

When they sinned shame shone a big spotlight on Adam and Eve and announced, "You're exposed!" Shame made them want to cover up and hide.

The enemy of your soul wants you to feel exposed and ashamed because he wants you to hide from the God who loves you and run away from the identity He has given you. That's why the enemy's voice so loudly accuses you: *You shouldn't have done that. You're so dumb. You should just keep your mouth closed. You're so ugly. Who would want to be with you?*

Shame tries to steer you away from the truth of who you are and the truth of who God is. Shame tells you that you must cover yourself, follow your own way, and trust in your own wisdom to compensate for your sin or your humanity.

But where shame exposes, love covers.

God could have scolded or further shamed Adam and Eve in the Garden of Eden, but instead He covered them. Genesis 3:21 says, "The Lord God made garments of skin for Adam and his wife, and clothed them" (NASB).

God covers you too, Gomer girl. He covers you with His love and forgiveness. He covers you with His strength and provision.

Here's something to think about: In order for God to cover Adam and Eve with animal skins, an animal had to be sacrificed. In the same way, a sacrifice was also required for our sin and shame to be covered. Jesus was that sacrifice.

Jesus' love covers our shame.
Jesus' life covers our sin.

Gomer girl, you are covered! You know the way you feel when you just don't want to face something? What do you usually want to do instead? I want to go hide in my closet or go back to bed and hide under the covers! But I'm a grown-up, so I can't hide under the covers...or can I? I can—and you can too! We can hide under the cover of God's perfect love. So the next time you feel isolated or exposed, instead of hiding behind good works or hiding in the false security of an idolotrinket, hide under the cover of God's acceptance and love.

Keep me as the apple of your eye; hide me in the shadow
of your wings…

Psalm 17:8

Shame Accuses

Okay, let's head back to the temple and continue the story of
the woman caught in adultery. When the scribes and the Pharisees
stood with the woman, they looked to Jesus to confirm their accusation: "In the Law Moses commanded us to stone such women;
what then do You say?" (John 8:5 NASB).

In other words the religious leaders were saying, "Okay, Jesus!
We've isolated this woman, exposed her, and now it's time for her
to feel the weight of our accusation. And we want You to give her
the ultimate punishment. *You* accuse her!"

So what do you think Jesus said?

Nothing. He was silent.

"Jesus stooped down and with His finger wrote on the ground"
(John 8:6 NASB). Not quite what you might expect, is it? We don't
know what Jesus wrote, but we do know this—the same finger
that wrote the law on tablets of stone atop Mount Sinai is the same
finger that wrote, and still writes, grace. Jesus easily could have
accused that woman of adultery. But only shame accuses. Jesus
gives grace.

The woman's story continues in verse 7: "But when they persisted in asking Him, He straightened up, and said to them, 'He
who is without sin among you, let him *be the first* to throw a stone
at her'" (NASB). Well, not a man in the crowd was without sin. So
instead of picking up stones to throw, they picked up their droopy,

disappointed faces and walked away. Shame can never speak louder than the voice of truth, and shame will never be stronger than the shelter of God's grace.

The woman must have been surprised as she stood there in the presence of Jesus, still isolated and exposed but not accused. John 8:10-11 says, "Straightening up, Jesus said to her, 'Woman, where are they? Did no one condemn you?' She said, 'No one, Lord.' And Jesus said, 'I do not condemn you, either. Go. From now on sin no more'" (NASB).

Oh, Gomer girl, Jesus is the lover of your soul. He doesn't accuse, but He also doesn't excuse. If Jesus had ignored that dear woman's sin, He would have been disregarding her value. Jesus loves each of us Gomer girls too much to let us get stuck in—and then stay in—a place where sin or selfishness has bound us to insecurity and eventual despair.

Sin enslaves you, but truth sets you free.

Drop the Rocks

Jesus could have picked up a rock that day and thrown it at the woman. Instead, He picked up grace and covered her.

If someone has been throwing rocks of judgment and condemnation at you, your soul may be bruised and tender. You might feel invisible—or even wish you *were* invisible. Or maybe you've been the one throwing rocks of judgment and condemnation at yourself. Gomer girl, you need to ask yourself a question: If Jesus doesn't condemn you, why are you condemning yourself? Jesus' words to the accused woman are the same words He speaks to you and me: *Go. From now on sin no more.* That's your permission to drop the rocks and pick up grace instead.

Shame condemns you, but Jesus took your shame and drank the cup of condemnation dry when He died for you on the cross. That shame is no longer your own. So shame off you!

> We can drop the rock of shame and go to the rock of our salvation.

Though Scripture describes Israel—and Gomer—as "swallowed up," "wandering alone," "like something no one wanted," and who "had sold herself," they were still wanted by God. His love never wavered. He said, "I will heal their waywardness and love them freely, for my anger has turned away from them" (Hosea 14:4). And those are His words to us too.

God doesn't want you to be swallowed up in sin or despair. He wants you to be swallowed up in His forgiveness. He doesn't want you to wander away from Him and be alone. He wants you to always be with Him. He doesn't want you to believe the lie that nobody wants you. He wants you to believe the truth that you are loved and wanted by Him. And He doesn't want you to sell yourself to cheap lovers who don't value you. Rather, He wants you to be sold out to—and for—Him.

Gomer girl, if you feel stuck on a slave block of your own making, don't get address labels made. The slave block is not your permanent home! God can always take what seems like a dead end and make a pathway to freedom out of it. He can take you from your lowest point and turn it into one of your best memories.

Your Valley of Achor: A Door of Hope

Can you imagine the emotions Gomer must have fought as she stood on that slave block? Standing there in chains, she may have been saying to herself, *Gomer, you blew it. You are beyond hope.*

But in Hosea 2:15, we hear a voice of truth: "Then I will give her her vineyards from there, and the valley of Achor as a door of hope" (NASB). God promises to make a valley of trouble into a door of hope! That awful slave block will not be Gomer's dead end. It will instead become a pathway to greater freedom.

Have you ever heard of the valley of Achor? If not, I'll tell you a little bit about it. When the Israelites, under the leadership of Joshua, entered the Promised Land, one of the first places they came upon was a valley near Jericho. The word *Achor* means "muddy" or "turbid" and may have been connected to the rolling waters of the Jordan River at flood stage.

In its early days, the valley of Achor was an entirely different place. Imagine a group of Israelite grandmas kneading bread dough and reminiscing about the good old days. One of their favorite topics would have been Achor. It's like your own fond memories of when you went away to college or moved into your first apartment. Perhaps you remember the stuffed peppers that were always served in the cafeteria or the ugly green couch you and your roommate bought at a garage sale. Like you recall those things, the Israelite grandmas recalled the churning Jordan at flood stage. Think of it as nostalgia—the memories are fond even though the reality wasn't always perfect.

If you've been married for a while, you probably can recall some rosy memories of your newlywed days. One of my Achor moments comes whenever I run my finger across the $35 wedding band that Phil gave me when I said, "I do." Phil has given me a new ring since then, and I don't wear the $35 band anymore, but I cherish it as a reminder of my wedding day and my life as a new bride.

Those are the sweet memories of the valley of Achor. Things may not have been perfect, but you recall those moments and images with fondness.

There was another side to the valley of Achor, though, and its memories are of a different variety. Joshua 7 recounts how Israel conquered Jericho. Their first steps into the Promised Land certainly conjured up sweet memories of victory. But then they attacked Ai—a little city, a big loss! This loss would result in bitter memories for the Israelites because their disobedience was the reason they lost the battle. So the valley of Achor evoked both memories of the good old days and also the days of shame, loss, and defeat.

We all have some valley of Achor memories, don't we? The most wonderful times in our lives can also bring back some of our worst memories. When I hold that $35 wedding band, I smile as I recall the early days of my marriage. But along with that I remember some ugly fights Phil and I had as young adults trying to adjust to married life. And those Achor memories don't make me smile at all!

Get the point of Achor? The bitter and the sweet of the valley represent promise followed by problems. Triumph followed by troubles. It's all of our stories, isn't it? Sterling silver always shines before it tarnishes. We say, "I do" before we say, "I do it my way." We first walk in faith before wandering off into unfaithfulness.

We receive our identity from God, and then we forget and try to achieve an identity on our own.

But there is an echo from Achor that you and I—just like wayward Israel and hopeless Gomer—can hear. God will always take the lowest point in our life—the time of spoiled potential, dashed hopes, and terrible shame—and turn it into a honeymoon of new beginnings.

Do you need God to turn your valley of Achor into a door of hope? Do you need Him to make the slave block into a stepping stone rather than a dead end? Oh, Gomer girl, He can. And He will!

You may feel like a woman caught in the very act of being human—stuck in sin, self, or insecurity—but you are caught in the loving arms of Jesus, and His love covers you. Jesus Himself is your door of hope, sweet Gomer girl! He loves, accepts, and completes you. It is through Him that you have a hope and a future. And it is not a future chained to defeat!

God will always redeem us. He will always buy us back from whatever enslaves us. Let's get going with the next part of the story. We're going to figure out how to get Gomer—and ourselves—off of that slave block!

12

The Buyback

I will deliver this people from the power of the grave...I will heal their waywardness and love them freely, for my anger has turned away from them.

HOSEA 13:14; 14:4

"Wanna do a concert in Lucedale?" my friend Lori said.

"*Where?*" I asked.

As it turned out, Lucedale, Mississippi, was the tiny town where Lori had grown up. This was back in 1988, and I'd just recorded a CD. Lori thought it would be great if I could sing at some churches in her hometown, so she proceeded to call uncles and aunts and cousins—and friends of uncles and aunts and cousins—until we had a whole Lucedale tour booked! We packed up our curling irons and shoulder-padded jackets and headed down the highway in Lori's van, singing along to "Don't Worry, Be Happy."

The plan was for me to sing and play songs from my CD while Lori ran the sound, a job that consisted of rotating ancient volume knobs on ancient sound boards in nearly ancient churches. But on one special night, I wasn't going to play a church concert. I was going to be singing in a coffee house. I felt so trendy and hip!

When we arrived at the coffee house, the manager warned me, "We could have a full house or nobody at all. I couldn't afford to advertise."

I told him it was no big deal. I was just grateful for the opportunity. And that was true. I *was* grateful for the opportunity—until the local winning Little League team and all of their family members busted through the front door! When I had begun my concert, the only people there were the manager, the barista, Lori, and a few of her friends. I had just finished my first song when in rushed the Little League crowd.

They were sweaty and loud, but I politely greeted them from the stage anyway. No one heard a word I said, of course. Lori turned up the volume, and I tried again. They still didn't respond. They just hooped and hollered even louder!

Lori pushed the play button, and the next track began. Playing the keyboard and singing along with the music, I faced an audience who I knew—even though I couldn't see them—wasn't looking at me. Trying to hide my humiliation, I just kept singing. I even told myself, *I have an audience of one. God is watching and listening.* But that didn't help at all! The longer I sang, the louder the Little Leaguers got, and the more invisible I felt.

I couldn't take it! So instead of singing the ten songs I had planned, I sang four. I said into the microphone, "For my last song, I want to sing a song I wrote called 'Someday.'" I prayed that Lori could hear me over the roar of the sugared-up, prepubescent boys. Evidently she did because soon enough I heard the track begin.

I took a deep breath and thought, *I can make it four and a half minutes longer!* I started playing and singing. And then suddenly I was done. Instead of facing the audience like a grown-up, semi-professional musician, I decided to leave them all behind me as the song suggested. I stopped playing the keyboard and kept singing with the track. And then slowly but surely, I turned around until I was singing to the back wall. Oh, my gosh! Can you believe I did that? I was so insecure that I couldn't bear to face an entire room of people who didn't even care I was there.

I was standing on a stage, but I was being ignored. I didn't want to be on display—I wanted to disappear.

I felt obvious and invisible all at the same time.

Oh, girl, if I felt like that in an obscure coffee house in a little town with a bunch of tween boys, how much more do you think our girl Gomer felt standing on the slave block in front of that crowd?

Put yourself in Gomer's chains. Feel her shame at that moment. Stand in her place on the slave block—humiliated, enslaved, hopeless.

I could leave the coffee house, but Gomer couldn't rescue herself. Her situation was hopeless until Hosea showed up to redeem her—to buy her back.

Undeserved

If cell phones had existed in Israel that day Gomer went up for sale, I can guarantee you that the towers would have been overloaded because everyone—and I mean E-V-E-R-Y-O-N-E—would have been on the phone!

Your super-chatty girlfriend would have called you and asked,

"Did you hear about Gomer? Do you think Hosea knows she's being sold? What do you think he'll do when he finds out? You should call him!"

"No way!" you would have answered. "You tell him yourself. He's not going to find out from me!"

But Hosea actually would have already found out about Gomer because he found out from God Himself. God called on him to redeem Gomer and told the heartbroken and betrayed husband, "Go, show your love to your wife again, though she is loved by another" (Hosea 3:1).

God told Hosea to go down to that dirty slave auction house and get Gomer back. And about Gomer having been loved by another? That may have been a ginormous understatement of biblical proportions! Likely, she had been loved by *many* others. But God didn't say, "Go show judgment to your wife" or "Go show your wife you're disappointed in her." God told Hosea to show love. Not condemnation or retribution. Love!

Hosea had been replaced and rejected, and now God was telling him to do the unthinkable—buy back his wayward wife and love her again.

We've been trying to see the "me" in Gomer and identify with her, but shift with me for a second. How would you feel if you were *Hosea* and had been asked to do such a thing? He must have felt betrayed, like it wasn't fair or right that he should be expected to buy back Gomer. It must have been incredibly humbling as well. And he must have had to stifle the urge to teach her a lesson.

At that moment maybe Hosea needed to love God more than he loved Gomer in order to obey. We can't forget that Hosea was not super-husband; he was human-husband. He *had* to feel hurt by Gomer's actions. He probably fought feelings of disgust. And certainly he felt embarrassed in front of the men of that town. He was a spiritual leader in the community, and his wife had left him to commit flat-out, in-your-face adultery over and over.

But Hosea had been called by God, and he followed God. And his willingness to obey probably gave him the strength to obey. And deep down, the romantic in me hopes—really hopes—that he still loved her. Don't you?

Even if he did still love her, was it really fair of God to ask Hosea to do such a thing? Gomer's behavior shouldn't have merited any love from him. She certainly didn't deserve to be redeemed, did she? What she deserved was to be left on that slave block alone, tasting the bitter fruit of her wayward heart.

But Hosea did not treat Gomer as her sin deserved. His love for her was not dependent on her love for him. His heart for Gomer echoed God's heart for Israel: "How can I give you up, O Ephraim? How can I surrender you, O Israel?...My heart is turned over within Me, all My compassions are kindled" (Hosea 11:8 NASB).

Did you know that God's heart for Israel is the same heart He has for you? No matter where you stand, He sees you. You may feel obvious and invisible all at the same time, stuck on a slave block of your own making—wrapped in chains of defeat, insecurity, or despair. But no matter where you are and how you got there, God wants you back. He says, "I have loved you with an everlasting love" (Jeremiah 31:3). And because of His amazing love, "he does not treat us as our sins deserve or repay us according to our iniquities" (Psalm 103:10).

Just like Hosea was willing to redeem Gomer, God is always willing to redeem you and me. The apostle Peter reminds us,

"...you were not redeemed with perishable things like silver or gold from your futile way of life inherited from your forefathers, but with precious blood, as of a lamb unblemished and spotless, *the blood* of Christ" (1 Peter 1:18-19 NASB). Another apostle, Paul, continues the message: "But because of his great love for us, God, who is rich in mercy, made us alive with Christ even when we were dead in transgressions—it is by grace that you have been saved" (Ephesians 2:4-5). And finally Jesus "gave Himself for us to redeem us from every lawless deed, and to purify for Himself a people for His own possession, zealous for good deeds" (Titus 2:14 NASB).

> God doesn't redeem you because
> you deserve it, but because
> His mercy dictates it. You aren't
> redeemed because you are worthy,
> but because you are worth it.

Valuable

Hosea didn't redeem Gomer because she was worthy, but because she was worth it. And so he went to the slave block to buy her back: "So I bought her for fifteen shekels of silver and about a homer and a lethek of barley" (Hosea 3:2).

Gomer had a price tag on her—about 30 pieces of silver—and

Hosea had to scrape his money and belongings together to come up with the equivalent. (That's probably why he added some barley to the mix.)

I can imagine Hosea, having just emptied his savings account and arriving at the market where the slave auction was being held. His heart must have been crushed to see the woman he cherished standing barely clothed before the crowd. And unlike the crowd, Hosea didn't consider what she could do but rather who she was. And he didn't see just *where* she was, he saw *whose* she was—his.

When the auctioneer opened the bidding, Hosea offered the first bid. Another bid was made, and Hosea upped his price. The bidding went on until Hosea offered his equivalent of 30 pieces of silver. The auctioneer's hammer fell as he pronounced, "Sold!" When Gomer glanced up to see who would be her new master, Gomer's eyes must have filled with tears—tears of shame and relief, tears of regret and uncertainty.

Can you imagine what Gomer must have been thinking and feeling? *Will he ever forgive me? Can he ever really accept and love me again?*

The clatter of the hammer and the word *sold* reverberated in her soul. *He rescued me? Hosea bought me back?* Her eyes stared at the dirty ground beneath her feet. Gomer knew, as everyone did back then, that 30 pieces of silver was the price of a slave. She had traded in her wedding band for the shackles of slavery. Gomer could not lift her chin as she heard his footsteps drawing nearer and nearer to where she stood. Trembling as the cold wind brushed her bare arms, she shook with hunger and fear.

Hosea made his way to the front of the room, gave the auctioneer a pouch of silver coins, and pointed to a heaping bag of barley sitting on the auction house floor. The auctioneer nodded, shoved the coins in his pocket, and pulled out a key. Then with one swift pull on the chain attached to Gomer's wrist, he unlocked the chain, and it clattered to the floor. Hosea reached for Gomer, yet she could not look into his eyes.

Lifting her dirty hand, Hosea brought it to his lips and tenderly kissed it. He then walked his wife off the slave block, covering her with his cloak and whispering in her ear, "You are to live with me many days; you must not be a prostitute or be intimate with any man, and I will behave the same way toward you" (Hosea 3:3).

Those are Hosea's statements that are recorded in Scripture, but I wonder if he said a lot more between those few sentences—the kind of words shared only between a husband and wife.

You Always Have My Heart

Even though Gomer may have been expecting to hear that she was now Hosea's slave instead of his wife, I wonder if he may have said something like this: "Gomer, I chose you once, and I choose you again. Don't let shame keep you from turning to me. I don't see what you've done; I see who you are—my beloved bride.

"Even when you're stained and tattered, you have my heart. Though I feel hurt and angry, I will never leave you. I will always be yours, even when you don't want to be mine. You may see my anger and disappointment, but my anger is born of love—deep, relentless love. The sorrow I feel from your rejection is never so great as to make me forget you. Your sin is ever before me, but so is your suffering and your weakness. I don't love you because of anything you have done. You cannot merit my love, and you cannot forfeit it either.

"My beloved, my affection toward you is so much stronger than the chains you wore. I willingly bore your shame when I redeemed you, and you now bear my name. How can I give you up? You were the bride I chose, and you will always be the bride I love. When I loved you, loveliness rose in you like the sun. You blossomed and became the beautiful bride I knew you always were.

"The wilderness has been no place for you. Let the water of my words refresh and bring you back to life. Come home, my beloved, for you are my bride. You were clothed with a radiant gown of purity, and it still fits you. Let me help you remove the ragged garment of your rebellion, for it does not bring out your beauty.

"You rejected my provision and went to other lovers to meet your needs. You disregarded the position of honor I placed you in and went to other places and people to find your prominence. Is it that you only want love you can earn? Do you only desire worth that you feel you deserve? Do you only think you are significant if you have achieved your own importance?

"Gomer, you are worthy and significant. I love and accept you, and when you embrace that truth, you will find the completeness you long for. You have been trying to become who you already were. You have been striving for what you already possess. You have been seeking what was already yours. Return with me and return to me. Reclaim what is yours in me. I have pulled you toward me with cords of love, not chains of condemnation. I don't want you wearing a yoke of slavery when you should be clothed in the garment of a beautiful bride.

"You are worth the cost of this redemption. I will always see you as beautiful, for you are mine. I will always think of you as lovable because I love you. So please cease striving to find your place, my precious Gomer. You have already been found in me."

Can you just let these words from Hosea to Gomer settle over you? And can you hear them as God's words to you?

No matter where we are, God sees who we are. We are His, and He loves us with an everlasting love.

Gomer girl, if you are enslaved to insecurity, God whispers, "You are safe in Me." If you are stuck in an identity crisis, God says, "You are found in Me." If you are chained by discontentment, God reassures, "You can be satisfied in Me." And if shame binds you, God affirms, "My love covers you."

God paid the ultimate price to purchase your freedom. He gave Jesus, "who loves us and released us from our sins by His blood" (Revelation 1:5 NASB). Ephesians 1:7 says, "In Him we have redemption through His blood, the forgiveness of our trespasses, according to the riches of His grace" (NASB).

God has redeemed us, and He can break any chains that bind us! Often we think of redemption as a one-time event, happening the moment we receive the forgiveness, cleansing, and life of Christ through faith. And that is true—when you receive Christ, you become a Christian and are redeemed. But, Gomer girl, God redeems you every day! He buys you back from the slavery of sin. He breaks the powerful chains of your own selfishness. He frees you from fear and releases you from guilt.

What Does Freedom Look Like?

Even when she had been set free, Gomer must have remembered what those chains felt like. Her before-and-after pictures were pretty clear—once in chains, free from chains. Our chains are just as gone as Gomer's were, but because they aren't tangible, we can forget that they're no longer on us. And sometimes we *live* like they're still on us. So let me give you a practical way to think about your chains—you know, the ones you *used* to wear.

Think of chains as Post-it notes, not superglue! You know the difference, right? A Post-it note sticks to your notebook, mirror, or cell phone case pretty well, doesn't it? It stays there until you remove it. If that little piece of paper were stuck to the same place with superglue, though, what would happen when you tried to remove it? You would tug and tug, and it wouldn't come off. If you pulled hard enough, some of the paper might rip off, but part of it would stay permanently glued to the surface to which it's attached.

When God redeems you, He sets you free. The sin you thought was superglued to your soul becomes a Post-it note. God peels it away and frees you from it. Feelings of insecurity, invisibility, and insignificance are no longer stuck to your soul. Lots of us Gomer girls—me being one of them—live like we have to drag around our chains. We don't need to, though, because they've been removed.

But wait! If they've been removed, why are those chains still around? Because we have the power to put them back on. It's our choice—chains or change.

What do you need God to free you from? You can begin the change right now! Grab a pad of Post-it notes and on each page write something you need to have God rescue, redeem, and free you from. (For example, I wrote down *self-awareness, insecurity,* and *comparison*.) Then stick those little squares to yourself. Really! Do it! When you do, you'll discover that it's hard to make them stick, and if they do stick, they won't stay long. Get the point? You're truly free from those things!

> Jesus turned everything that was once superglued to us into Post-it notes!

Sure, we can put the Post-it notes on us over and over again, but they're not permanent. They keep falling off. It takes effort to keep those things attached to us!

Do this every morning if you need to, Gomer girl. Write what you need God to redeem you from on Post-it notes and stick them on yourself as you're getting dressed, eating breakfast, driving to work, or running errands. As you see how easily they fall off you, you'll be reminded that you are not bound—you are free. You are free to be the beloved! The things you wrote on those Post-it notes are not your identity.

I hope that Post-it notes are constantly falling off you like a ticker-tape parade! As they fall like a million raindrops, I hope you feel the cleansing that this act represents. When you see one fall off, stomp on it and say, "I am not how I feel! Sin is not the boss of me! God set me free, and I am free indeed! I am not what I struggle with! I am not my past!"

Gomer girl, this is so true—we are free! We are not stuck in sin or self-defeating habits unless we stick with them and therefore stick them to ourselves. We are free! The things we struggle with don't have to define us. God can use everything to *refine* us.

He Redeems and Restores

Just like Hosea freed Gomer, God has freed us too. He has freed us from the chains that bind us. He has freed us from the power of our sin. He has freed us from the influence of our past and our struggles. God redeems *everything*. And what He redeems, He restores.

Remember what God said to the Israelites about their restoration? "Then I will give her her vineyards from there, and the valley of Achor as a door of hope. And she will sing there as in the days of her youth, as in the day when she came up from the land of Egypt" (Hosea 2:15 NASB).

Just as God wanted to make everything new for Israel and turn their worst memories and lowest places into a "door of hope," so did Hosea want Gomer to feel the newness and the redemption of his restoration and love. He wanted Gomer to sing again as she had in the days of her youth—like in the early days when she had first fallen in love with Hosea.

Do you remember those early days when you first met Christ? Can you recall the wonder, the newness? I don't know about you, but for me it was easy to *phroneo* back then. It wasn't hard to keep my affection set on things above and my focus on Jesus. I couldn't wait to read the Bible and hear what God was saying to me—little me! I was far more God-aware than self-aware. And it was sweeter then. Can you relate?

God wants to bring us back to those moments. We always seem to find ourselves in such a human cycle, though. We get off to a great start. And then we fizzle out. Promise and potential—*kerplunk!*—hit the wall of failure. We desire to stay close to God, but we become distracted and stray from Him. Redeemed. Regress! Our freedom of choice turns to the frustration of chains. But God redeems everything.

God's redemptive touch, though, is not confined to the present or even to the future. God's work in our lives renews everything that has come before—our best days and our worst days.

Let's visit another prophet to see how this redemption and renewing works. Joel used a locust plague as his sermon illustration in the same way Hosea used his marriage as a sermon illustration. (I'm not suggesting that a marriage partner and locusts have anything in common. *Wink!*) In Joel 2:25, God promises, "I will repay you for the years the locusts have eaten."

All of us have places in our lives where the "locusts" have eaten. Our hopes have been dashed, mistakes have been made, and loss upon loss has piled up. But God promises He will repay all that damage. And what do you think God means when He says He will repay?

The Hebrew word we translate as "repay" in Joel 2:25 is *shalam*. Sound familiar? What word comes to mind when you see *shalam*? Yep, I heard you. *Peace.* That's what I think of too. But according to *Accordance* (Bible software), this word *shalam* means "to be safe (in mind, body, or estate); figuratively, to be (causatively, make) completed." So God promises us two things: First, He will make us safe from past damage. And second, He will make it—and us—complete.

When Gomer said "I do" to Hosea, she became the beloved bride. She was made complete. Her past was overwritten by her present. And when she strayed and became enslaved, Hosea redeemed her and made her safe—even from past damage.

The idea that God completes our past helps me understand Romans 8:28 even better. That verse says that God makes all things work together for the good of those who love Him, right?

My friend, that means God works *all* things together—including your past damage—for good. Your failures, your weakness, your selfishness, your insecurity, your discontent—God takes all that and uses it all for your ultimate good!

Sweet Gomer girl, you may have endured something so awful in your past that you can't even imagine God redeeming and restoring *shalom*—or peace—to you. But His promise is true. What the enemy stole, He will *shalam*. What selfish people have taken from you, God will repay. Even the damage you may have inflicted on yourself through your own choices, God can redeem.

Hosea said that God would restore Gomer—and Israel—so they would respond as they had in their youth. Joel promised that God would repay what had been taken away and make everything both safe and complete. Paul said that all things work together for our good. Even the prophet Job, who had lost everything—children, home, wife, money, health—was eventually blessed beyond everything he'd lost: "So the LORD blessed Job in the second half of his life even more than in the beginning" (Job 42:12 NLT).

God may not replace what you have lost, but He will repay it. He will *shalam* and you will experience *shalom*.

There's a verse, Genesis 50:20, that I speak to my past, and you too can speak its truth to your past damages and losses. Seriously, sister! You may even need to stand up, turn around as if you are addressing your past, and quote this truth: "You intended to harm me, but God intended it for good to accomplish what is now being done." Excellent! Now, say it again! "You intended to harm me, but God intended it for good to accomplish what is now being done."

Good job! I'm cheering you on and saying it right along with you. Gomer girl, you are not your past! You are not what happened to you. You are not your bad habits. You are not your struggles. You are not your fear or insecurity. You are not those rusty old chains that once bound you. You are not someone else's opinion of you.

You are loved, accepted, and complete. You are the beloved. So tell your past where it belongs—behind you! And those old shackles? They are not the boss of you. God will *shalam* and *shalom*. He literally will help you make peace with your past.

In my favorite C.S. Lewis book, *The Great Divorce*, the author has an imaginary conversation with one of his heroes, George MacDonald, as they sit together just outside of heaven. MacDonald tells Lewis, "Son...ye cannot in your present state understand eternity...That is what mortals misunderstand. They say of some temporal suffering, 'No future bliss can make up for it,' not knowing that Heaven, once attained, will work backwards and turn even that agony into a glory."

What my favorite dead author is saying is that even your most agonizing loss—even your worst day—will be cast in the light of *shalam*. It will be redeemed and restored as all things are made new.

Gomer girl, it is for freedom that Christ has set us free! So let's stand firm and not ever again submit to a yoke of slavery because God redeems, restores, and repays.

God did not
redeem me
because I am
worthy,
but because He thinks I am
worth it.

13

The Boundaries That Keep You Free

"When that day comes," says the LORD, "you
will call me 'my husband' instead of 'my
master.'...I will make you my wife forever,
showing you righteousness and justice,
unfailing love and compassion. I will be
faithful to you and make you mine, and
you will finally know me as the LORD."
HOSEA 2:16,19-20 NLT

When our oldest son, Clayton, left for college, we got a little shih tzu puppy named Lucy. (It sounds like we were trying to replace Clayton, but we weren't!) Lucy is a furry little dust mop of a creature covered with black and white hair. When the weather is cold, she's content to just lie on the couch in front of the fireplace for about 13 hours a day. But when spring arrives, she wants to be outside! The problem is we don't have a fenced backyard. And because we know she has wayward potential, Lucy is always on the end of a leash when she's outside—most of the time with a human attached to the other end.

In the spring, Lucy wants to be outdoors far more than we humans have time for, so we've attached the end of her leash to various items in the backyard. She's been tethered to the wrought-iron bench under the oak tree, the post on the back porch, and even the garden hose.

I'd been telling Phil that we needed to fence our backyard since Lucy was about three months old, but my requests just fell upon the rocky soil of excuses—too expensive, trees in the way, weather too bad, and so forth. No matter that I'd begun to refer to it as a "boundary of bliss." (Okay, okay! *I'm* the one who needs a fence!)

It reached the point of insanity. If I wasn't outside with Lucy, I was listening to her mournful moans as she panted at the back door. So again I mentioned to Phil, "We must get a fence! I can't take this whining and begging much longer." (Yes, I was hoping that he would be unable to take *my* whining and begging much longer too!) My husband just muttered another excuse, stroked the dog, and said, "Lucy, you be a good girl!" Then it was off to work for him—and back to the leash for me. Resigned to my fate once again, I took the mopey little girl into the backyard where I leashed her to the end of the garden hose, told her to have fun, and went back inside.

About half an hour later, the phone rang. It was not unlike phone calls I'd received in the past: "Ma'am, I think I've found your dog."

My first instinct was to retort, "No, my dog is in the backyard tied to the garden hose because my frugal husband won't get a fence—and I'm on the verge of insanity!" But that was TMI, so instead I listened to how Lucy had been found in this lady's garage, attached to a garden hose, and with her face crammed into a bag of dog food that she'd chewed her way through.

"Oh, my gosh! I'm so so sorry!" I gasped. Mortified, I sent our youngest son, Connor, to bring Lucy back home.

How did Lucy ever disconnect the hose? I wondered. I imagined her maneuvering her little body under the spigot, twisting herself in pretzel-like motions, and somehow managing to unscrew the hose. I went outside to investigate and discovered that the garden hose was still attached to the spigot. I was totally confused. *This would not have happened if we had a fence!* I fumed. *I need a fence! This is so embarrassing!*

Soon enough along came Connor and happy-go-lucky Lucy with a leash and garden hose attached to her collar. She was too cute and tangled to scold, so I simply unattached her and sent her back inside. It was then that I discovered we actually had *two* garden hoses in the backyard—one attached to the spigot and one that had been attached to Lucy!

Lucy had wandered the neighborhood dragging a 12-foot garden hose—the Rothschild ambassador of irresponsibility. *The whole neighborhood must think we are the worst pet owners ever!* I thought. *Who attaches their dog to an unattached garden hose and then lets her roam the neighborhood? Phil thinks a fence is too expensive? Well, I can guarantee it's cheaper than therapy!*

Yes, boundaries can be restrictive, but sometimes they are a loving gift to us. They make us secure and prevent us from wandering away. And that's why the very first thing Hosea gave Gomer after he freed her was a boundary.

Bonds of Love

As Hosea walked Gomer out of the auction house the day he freed her, he whispered, "You must live with me many days." He drew a boundary. And he could draw boundaries because he first drew Gomer with love.

Hosea drew Gomer back to himself with love, not judgment, just as God drew His wayward people back to Him: "I led them with cords of a man, with bonds of love, and I became to them as one who lifts the yoke from their jaws; and I bent down *and* fed them" (Hosea 11:4 NASB).

The imagery is beautiful, isn't it? God treats us tenderly, and Hosea treated Gomer tenderly also. Hosea uses the words "cords of a man" and "bonds of love" to describe how God drew Israel. He refers to a string you would use to guide a child, not a rope you would use to pull an animal. Hosea treated Gomer, his wife, with tenderness—not like a substandard slave. Remember, Hosea paid the price of a slave for Gomer. Yet he didn't want her to call him "master."

God wants the same from us. Let's look at Hosea 2:16 again: "'In that day,' declares the LORD, 'you will call me "my husband"; you will no longer call me "my master."'"

God wants you to see Him as the lover of your soul, not the gruff master who bosses you around. Unlike some ancient understanding of husband and wife—where the husband is the owner and the wife is the property—God is saying, "You are My beloved, and I am your ultimate Love."

God is the lover of your soul, and He wants to be not only Master and Lord but much more than that to you. He wants you to love Him and enjoy Him like He loves and enjoys you. God delights in you like an artist delights in his creation. He is capti-vated by you and proud of you. He cares for you like a father cares for his little girl, or like a knight cares for his lady. He wants to shel-ter and protect you like a mother bear protects her cub. His heart for you is so much more than you could ever imagine!

If I were Gomer, though, I would expect to call Hosea "mas-ter." I would not expect to show up back at home and resume my rightful place. I would expect to sleep in the guest room and endure months—or even years—of mistrust. After all that's what I deserve, isn't it?

It's in our nature to expect punishment. We don't expect grace when we blow it. We expect to be scolded.

Can You Scold Me Right Now?

"Can you scold me right now?" Those were Connor's words as he dragged his feet into the living room at 9:00 one night.

"Connor!" I growled. "You are a bad boy!" Of course, I was kid-ding—just trying to play along with him.

"Thanks," he said. "I just remembered I have homework!"

When I asked if he was serious—given the late hour—he replied in a grave tone of voice, "Totally."

I think Connor expected a real scolding at that point, but instead I just laughed and told him to shower fast and then he could knock it out. He headed for the shower without a genuine scolding, punishment, or even correction. Why was that? Because I didn't care about our bedtime/homework standard? By no means!

I laughed instead of scolding Connor because he delighted me. Of course, sometimes I do need to discipline him as an act of love, but on this night no punishment was needed. He was just a kid who'd forgotten his homework—a kid caught in the act of being human.

We often expect God to come to the slave block to rescue us, shake His head with disappointment, and then—as He walks us away—pull out the stone tablets from Mount Sinai and point to the commandments we have violated. If we feel that way, how much more would Gomer have felt? I bet she was ready for a tongue-lashing—ready to be treated like a slave.

But here was Hosea's response: "I am now going to allure her; I will lead her into the wilderness and speak tenderly to her" (Hosea 2:14). Wow—what a response!

God leads us with cords of love, and He speaks to us with tenderness. He doesn't harshly scold. He speaks to your heart with love. If we only think of God as a master who will punish us, then all God has is our duty and discipline. And He wants more than that. God wants your heart—not just your head and your hands—because if He has your heart, He has you.

That's why He draws us to Himself with bonds of love. *Love.* Not condemnation, but love. And often love shows up in the form of boundaries.

Boundaries That Protect

Hosea told Gomer, "Live with me many days. Do not be a prostitute or be with any other man, and I will do the same" (see Hosea 3:3).

Those words from Hosea reflect a boundary. The *New Living Translation* states it this way: "Then I said to her, 'You must live in my house for many days and stop your prostitution. During this time, you will not have sexual relations with anyone, not even with me.'"

Other translations of the Bible express that Hosea was telling Gomer that she would no longer step out on him and that he too would remain faithful. Either way, forever faithfulness and/or temporary abstinence are reasonable boundaries that reflect love. It is loving to draw boundaries because they protect us and grant us a sense of belonging as well as a sense of security.

A famous playground experiment illustrates the security that boundaries bring. In the experiment, a group of children were released from their classroom to play on the playground. When a sturdy chain-link fence surrounded the schoolyard, the kids moved about freely, playing as if they didn't have a care in the world. But when the fence was removed, the children clumped together in small groups, staying near the middle of the playground. Without the fence in place, they appeared confused and disoriented and didn't venture far.*

Without boundaries, the children were insecure. And without boundaries, we too are insecure. If God doesn't draw us to Himself with bonds of love and cords of a man, our thought processes demonstrate this insecurity. *Am I loved?* we wonder. *Am I worth it? Does God even see me? Am I valuable to Him? Do I have any significance?*

If Gomer didn't matter to Hosea, he wouldn't have set any type of boundary for her. He wouldn't have cared enough to first redeem her and then restrict her. The boundary may have been to prohibit her from going back to her old behavior, but it was ultimately to protect her heart.

---

* Robert J. Morgan, *Nelson's Complete Book of Stories, Illustrations & Quotes,* (Nashville: Thomas Nelson Publishers, 2000), 592-93.

Boundaries are not to punish us.
They are to protect us.

God doesn't want us Gomer girls to be hurt by our wandering ways. His boundaries are not to prevent our happiness, but to instead protect our hearts.

Don't Let Anything Take Away Your Heart

Hosea explains that there are two boundaries we should pay special attention to: "Promiscuity, wine, and new wine take away one's *understanding*" (Hosea 4:11 HCSB).

That verse has an interesting Hebrew word *leb*, which is translated as "understanding." It means understanding of the heart—or the center—of something. Promiscuity and excessive wine can confuse your heart, getting into the center of your soul and touching places that shouldn't be messed with. The result is loss—the loss of part of your heart. To "take away your heart" doesn't mean stealing your heart as we would say today. ("Oh, that little pooch with the garden hose attached to her collar—she's so cute! She just stole my heart!") It actually means to take away your *understanding* or to remove you from something that should never have been taken.

We were created to have, as the deepest reality in our lives, a love relationship with Jesus. When we have that, everything else makes sense and flows from that relationship. But Hosea says that certain things—in this case promiscuity and wine—can erode the very center of our being. I don't know why Hosea chose to point out these two things as choices that can "take away your heart," but it makes perfect sense that they are two boundaries every Gomer girl should have.

I struggled with how personal I could—or should—get when it came to these two subjects, but as a fellow Gomer girl and sister in Christ, I want to love you with the grace and truth of Jesus. So, here goes! Let's tackle promiscuity first.

Promiscuity

Promiscuity is defined as "having casual or indiscriminate sexual relations with different partners before, or outside of, marriage." Now, if you're a married woman reading this book, you might be tempted to think, *Finally! Here's something in this book that's not about me!* Or you may be single and celibate and share the relief of the married reader. But promiscuity isn't just an act—it's also an attitude.

Let's get real here. Promiscuity isn't just having sex or going too far before or outside of marriage. Girl, promiscuity can take other forms too. If you've ever watched a movie with scenes that would embarrass you if your pastor walked into the room, chances are that movie is taking away your heart. If you read a book that caused you to think things about men you wouldn't want anyone else to know you're thinking, you're dealing with promiscuous thinking that will take away your understanding.

Sister, there are not 50 shades of gray when it comes to this subject. It is black-and-white. If it seems gray to you, that may be because your heart—and therefore your understanding—has been taken. So please value yourself enough to think and pray about this. God wants to protect your heart!

Ultimately promiscuity is an action. If you can identify with the definition of it given at the beginning of this section, sweet friend, this is God's heart toward you: Do not give yourself away to anyone but your husband. When you do give yourself to your husband, it needs to be after the ring is on your finger. (And I don't mean just the engagement ring!) Anything else is promiscuity, and promiscuity will cloud your thinking, muddle your emotions, and eventually take away your understanding—as well as your heart.

It's pretty common in this day and age to think of purity as an old-fashioned, outdated concept. I know many young Christian adults who sleep together or move in together when they are in a supposedly committed relationship. Oh, girl, it doesn't matter how committed you think you are—it's still promiscuity, and it can still take away your heart. And the simplest reason it takes away your heart is because it is sin.

Sin hurts you, reduces your value, and dishonors your future husband (which is true even if the man you're sleeping with is to become your husband). The Bible teaches sexual purity, but even secular studies have proven that promiscuity can lead to ineffective relationships, issues with self-concept, and even depression.

Here's the deal: Purity is never, ever—no, not ever!—a bad choice, and promiscuity is *always* the wrong choice. I think the biggest reason why promiscuity takes your heart is because it goes against God's perfect design of love that protects your heart.

Now, I am incredibly aware that—and totally sympathetic if—you may have just read this and thought, *Great! I'm not a virgin, and it's too late for me because I've given away something I can't get back.*

Dear one, please hear me. I wrote this for the woman who is dabbling in promiscuity or who is ignorant about its costs. If you have made the choice to be promiscuous in the past, please read 1 John 1:9, Romans 8:1, and Isaiah 43:18-19. Confess your sin, and God will cleanse you. He does not condemn you, so please don't condemn yourself. And don't dwell on the past. Dwell in the present truth that God makes all things new! If promiscuity has taken your heart, God can give you a sparkling new, restored one. Remember what the prophet Joel taught us? God can *shalam*—repay or restore—what the locusts destroyed.

So break that chain that binds you by establishing a boundary that will free you. The purity boundary gives you the liberty to celebrate who you are in Christ, guard your incredible value, and find ultimate satisfaction in the Lover of your soul.

Perhaps you need to start establishing a purity boundary by cleaning off your bookshelf and getting rid of the titles that take away your heart. Or maybe you need to stop viewing movies with sex scenes or nudity in them so as not to reduce your own value—or the value of the sisters who diminish themselves by displaying themselves as objects of lust rather than beloved women of God. If you're in a season of life where sexual activity outside of marriage is a temptation or a possibility, set a boundary to protect yourself from getting into a situation you'll regret. Your drive for sex is good, natural, and God-given—and that's why you need to guard it from taking you places that will take away your heart. You know what I mean, Gomer girl! If you live alone, do not invite a man inside to spend time alone with you. You don't need me to explain why! Also choose your clothes to reflect that you are a woman who knows her value and doesn't need to see herself reflected in the lustful eyes of a man.

Only you know which boundaries you need. And if you're unsure, talk to a friend or a more mature Christian woman. Oh, girl, don't let anything take away your heart!

Too Much Wine

Hosea gets gut-honest and in our faces about promiscuity, but he also says that too much wine will take our hearts away too. I don't think he's making us choose between drinking or not drinking. I think his point is that anything that impairs your ability to think clearly—or recognize your personal dignity and value to God—will take away your heart. That's why Paul advises the church in Ephesus not to be drunk with wine but instead to be filled with the Holy Spirit (see Ephesians 5:18).

Sure, the Bible warns against excess when it comes to wine, but even secular studies agree. Researchers have found that alcohol consumption—even on a single occasion—can throw off the delicate balance of our brain chemistry. Alcohol-related disruptions to our brain's chemical balance can trigger mood and behavioral changes, such as depression, feelings of agitation, and memory loss.

Anything that modifies or alters our mental clarity can take away our understanding, but being filled with God's Spirit will never take away your heart. You are God's beloved, so let His Spirit fill you. Now, I'm not promoting legalism when it comes to alcohol consumption. I'm promoting wisdom and godliness in any choice we make. I'm less concerned with a woman's choice to drink wine (in a responsible and spiritually thoughtful way) and far more concerned with nothing taking away her heart. Your heart is a beautiful thing to God, and He desires to protect it.

Is this a boundary you need? I'll be honest. It's a boundary I choose to keep because I know my tendency toward becoming addicted to things—even coffee and chocolate! And when I cross my boundaries, it will easily take away my understanding and impact my heart.

Search Your Soul

The main question we need to ask ourselves is this: How can Hosea's teaching on this help me to live today with Jesus as the center of my life?

Gomer girl, we are all prone to wander. Even though God redeems us, frees us, and empowers us to be the beloved, we can still stray.

Hosea says a "spirit of promiscuity" leads us to stray and disobey (see Hosea 4:12). Now, I wouldn't say that I struggle with a spirit of promiscuity. I don't deal with temptation in the sexual area. I put up a boundary years ago, and that boundary has protected me. But when I think about Hosea's words, I think I do struggle—I think we all do.

A spirit of promiscuity can show up in that desire for something "other" or something "bigger" or something that will make me feel seen or desired. It sprouts when I'm not feeling secure in Christ, and it can send me down a wayward path. Even if it doesn't manifest itself literally with sexual temptation, a spirit of promiscuity can show up in other ways—like unrestrained indulgence or seeking pleasure for pleasure's sake with no thought to honoring God in the process. I think that's because a spirit of promiscuity and the flesh are first cousins!

When I was reading Romans 8:5-7, I discovered that our flesh and a spirit of promiscuity have a lot in common. I decided to rephrase verses 5 and 6 by replacing the word "flesh" with the phrase "spirit of promiscuity." See if you agree how similar they are!

> Those who have a spirit of promiscuity have their minds set on what the spirit of promiscuity desires; but those who live in accordance with the Spirit have their minds set on what the Spirit desires. The mind governed by the spirit of promiscuity is death, but the mind governed by the Spirit is life and peace.

I hope that helped things make more sense to you! It sure did for me. And I know this—I do not want the spirit of promiscuity to lead me anywhere! Gomer girl, anything like promiscuity or any mood-altering substance takes away our hearts and leads us away from God. When our flesh is bent on wandering away from God and toward ourselves for satisfaction, we will wonder who we are. That's why we need boundaries to protect us.

Perhaps we need to ask ourselves some soul-searching questions:

- Is what I'm doing drawing me to—or away from—God?

- Are the things I think about bringing me life and peace, or are my thoughts killing me and creating chaos?

- Am I led by the Spirit of God or the spirit of promiscuity?

- Do my activities "take away my heart" or enrich my soul?

Three Boundaries to Set

As I'm learning how to identify with my identity and find myself in God's view of me, I am learning that boundaries help me. They protect me from straying into errors or lies. Boundaries help me stay close to God and my true identity. They also help me agree with who I am instead of always falling for how I feel. I've set up three major boundaries for myself, and I'd like to take you through each one.

> The love that sets boundaries is the love that sets us free.

Truth

The first boundary I've set for myself is *truth*. God's Word—the Bible—is truth. And if I stay within the boundary of His Word, trusting it and following it, I won't feel insecure because I will know the truth that keeps me safe from lies or feelings that go haywire. Psalm 119:11 says, "I have hidden your word in my heart that I might not sin against you."

That verse has many layers of meaning. First, Jesus Christ is the Word become flesh. He is the living Word of God. He lives within me, and His presence protects me from straying. And His written, holy Word is hidden in my heart. As I memorize it and meditate upon it, no matter what else is going on in my life, I have a resource that reminds me who I am and what I have in Christ. Psalm 119:133 also helps me focus upon truth: "Direct my footsteps according to your word; let no sin rule over me."

Other-Centeredness

If I stay within the boundary of *other-centeredness*, I won't feel invisible because I won't be so focused on myself. When my eyes are on others instead of on me, I'm happier because I am less self-aware.

When I was a painfully self-aware teenager—especially with my white cane—my mom would always remind me to focus on others. "Look into their eyes and ask them about themselves," she would tell me. "That way, all they see is your caring eyes, and all they are thinking about is how kind you are to them."

My mother was right, of course. And the added benefit of following her advice was that I would temporarily forget about myself when I was focused on someone else. Philippians 2:3 says, "Do nothing out of selfish ambition or vain conceit. Rather, in humility value others above yourselves."

Accountability

My third boundary, *accountability*, is my willingness to be responsible to another person—to tell her the truth and to live honestly and responsibly in relationship with her. When I choose to isolate myself, it's easy for me to become wise in my own eyes. But that's not necessarily true! "The way of a fool is right in his own eyes, but a wise man is he who listens to counsel" (Proverbs 12:15 NASB).

Accountability provides protection from me acting out of my iddiction and following Gomerisms. It keeps the truth before me. And when I live within the boundary of accountability, I'm encouraged and sharpened. As Proverbs 27:17 says, "Iron sharpens iron, so one man sharpens another" (NASB).

Accountability also demands honesty, and being honest with another person requires that I am honest with myself. James tells us to "confess your sins to one another, and pray for one another" (James 5:16 NASB), and the writer of Hebrews says, "Let us consider how to stimulate one another to love and good deeds" (Hebrews 10:24 NASB). And finally, accountability brings encouragement: "Therefore encourage one another and build up one another" (1 Thessalonians 5:11 NASB).

When I'm feeling insecure...or invisible...or discontent...or insignificant, it clues me in that I've chosen to stray from the safety of the boundaries God has provided. God's boundaries exist to protect your heart. They aren't meant to be burdensome—they're meant to bring you life. And here's another really great thing—He can place those boundaries in pleasant places.

Pleasant Places

When we think of boundaries, we don't necessarily think of pleasant places, do we? We think of a barbed-wire fence or a cement wall. But the boundaries God has given us are pleasant places.

God has lovingly placed us within the boundary of His covenant, which is a place of identity, security, and wholeness. And we have a delightful inheritance of satisfaction, peace, and purpose within these boundaries. The psalmist wrote, "The boundary lines have fallen for me in pleasant places; surely I have a delightful inheritance" (Psalm 16:6). The boundaries God sets for us are the bonds of love God uses to draw us in and keep us close to Him.

The English words "line" and "cord" both come from the Hebrew word *cheble*, which also means "measuring line," "territory," or "tied together." Think about that for a minute!

God has given you boundary lines in your life, and those boundary lines are created with cords of love! Imagine those boundary lines as drawn in the shape of a heart because they are another reminder of His love for you. All throughout the book of Hosea, the prophet expresses himself through Hebrew parallelism, a poetic tool writers use to say the same thing twice but with different words. For instance if I were writing a poem about my dog Lucy, I might say, "My wayward wanderer, my meandering mutt." Get the idea?

Well, you're going to love this! Hosea used Hebrew parallelism when he wrote "bonds of love" and "cords of a man." Can you think of how those two statements might be saying the same thing?

> God draws boundaries
> to draw us close.

If God "drew us with the cords of a man," who could that man possibly be? Yep, you got it—Jesus Christ! Mark 10:45 says, "The

Son of Man did not come to be served, but to serve, and to give his life as a ransom for many."

God draws each of us to Himself through the "cords of a man"— the Son of man. And if He is lifted up, He will *draw* all men—and all Gomer girls—to Himself (sec John 12:32). Oh, Gomer girl, God loves you *that* much! He loves you enough to draw you to Himself with Jesus Himself. And He will keep you close because He will never leave you or forsake you.

My fellow Gomer girl, let's stay close to God's heart so nothing can ever take away our own hearts. I know that you—like me— want to live like the beloved, so let's stay within the loving boundaries God has drawn for us. Let His love draw you in and keep you right next to His heart. When you live within the boundary of truth, you will always know who you are—and *whose* you are— the loved, accepted, and complete beloved of God!

The love that sets

boundaries

is the love that sets me

free.

#TheInvisibleBook

If You Ain't Got *Yada*,
You Ain't Got Nada

So let us know, let us press on to know the
LORD. His going forth is as certain as the
dawn; and He will come to us like the rain,
like the spring rain watering the earth.

HOSEA 6:3 NASB

If you watched sitcoms in the late '90s, you may recognize the
word *yada*. Made famous by the hit show *Seinfeld, yada* was first
uttered in the episode titled "The Yada Yada" by one of the characters—George's new girlfriend—who filled her stories with that
expression. She'd start a story, gloss over the middle of it with the
words *yada yada yada*, and then wrap up the story.

After meeting the girlfriend, Jerry says to George, "I noticed
she's big on the phrase *yada yada*,"

George asks, "Is *yada yada* bad?"

"No," Jerry answers. "*Yada yada* is good. She's very succinct."

After George contemplates the answer and agrees, Jerry finishes, "Yeah, it's like you're dating *USA Today*."

Ever since *yada*'s pop culture debut, we've been saying *yada yada yada* when we want to cut out parts of a story or avoid incriminating or excessive details. *Yada* is more than a filler or placeholder for more important words, though. It's the most important word of this book—seriously! *Yada* is actually a Hebrew word that means "to know."

And *yada* is what God desires most from us! If you and I are to live like the beloved we are, the only way to do this is to *yada* God. And that doesn't mean just knowing *about* Him. We really, really need to *know* Him. Let's revisit the opening scene of this book, the one where I am at the lake straying from God and my identity. Part of the reason I strayed was because I didn't *yada* God. Part of the reason Gomer and Israel strayed was because they didn't truly know who they were, and that's because they didn't really know God. Now, you may be thinking, *Huh? Sure, they knew God!* But the word *know* can be used in several ways. It can mean an informational knowing, but it can also mean an intimate knowing. God wants *yada*—the intimate knowing—from us.

Yada is the most intimate knowing we can experience. It means far more than simply knowing information. It brings to mind images of trust, passion, compassion, vulnerability, affection, exclusivity, and love.

Ultimately, it's a lack of knowledge that makes us prone to wander, and that's why *yada* is the most important word in this book. It's the most important action we can take to keep us from straying. Remember what happens when we wander? We become our own idol and get enslaved by sin and self.

Hosea teaches, "My people are destroyed from lack of knowledge" (Hosea 4:6). Gomer's story proves how true that is, for what you don't know can not only hurt you—it can also destroy you. I know that when I lack knowledge of God, my sense of identity and value are both destroyed. When I don't know who God really is, I have no idea who I am. When I don't *yada* God, my sense of security begins to wane, and my confidence slowly diminishes.

When we don't know God, we cannot know ourselves—and so we stray from God to find ourselves. We seek significance in our performance. We become overly self-aware and start to compare. We try to feel accepted by belonging to the right crowd. We attempt to make up for what is lacking in us by competing with others and trying to be better than they are. We strive and we sacrifice...and the list goes on and on and on (*yada yada yada!*).

But what God wants most from us is not our perfect performance or our best behavior. He also doesn't want our righteous reputation or disciplined sense of duty.

He wants our *yada*.

In fact, God desires our loyal love for and knowledge of Him far more than He wants our sacrifices or offerings (see Hosea 6:6). Why? Because to know Him—to really, really know Him—is to love Him. And when we love Him, we don't leave Him.

This chapter opened with Hosea 6:3 (NASB), but it's so important that I'm going to say it again: "So let us know, let us press on to know the LORD. His going forth is as certain as the dawn; and He will come to us like the rain, like the spring rain watering the earth." Oh, Gomer girl, if we want to know who we are and live like God's beloved, we "press on" to know Him!

God, the Lover of your soul, says to you—His sweet Gomer

girl—"I will betroth you to Me forever; yes, I will betroth you to Me in righteousness and in justice, in lovingkindness and in compassion, and I will betroth you to Me in faithfulness. Then you will know the LORD" (Hosea 2:19-20 NASB).

God pursues us so we will know him. So in order to know God, we must respond to His gracious pursuit. But ultimately we know Him—we *yada* Him—through His Word.

Knowing His Word

In Hosea's day, the Word of God had become irrelevant. The people had disregarded God's law and consequently degraded His love and their own identity. Because they didn't know God's Word, they didn't know God, and they didn't know their own value.

In Hosea 8:12, God says, "I wrote for them the many things of my law, but they regarded them as something foreign." The people in Hosea's day chose to ignore God's Word. They didn't listen to the truth, so they didn't *know* the truth. And when we don't know—or *yada*—the truth, the truth cannot set us free. According to John 8:32, we will live enslaved to lies and insecurity if we are ignorant of God's Word.

My fellow Gomer girl, here's what we need to internalize: We are only ignorant of His Word when we ignore it. You don't need a seminary degree to know God's Word—you just need willingness. God will show you His truth in every verse if you are simply willing to open your Bible and read it. If you overlook it, I can guarantee you'll feel invisible. So treat God's Word as a treasure because it is—it's His gift to you. It's the way to knowing Him and knowing yourself.

When we think little of God's truth, we
will eventually think little of ourselves.

The Israelites treated God's Word as something "foreign." When
we consider God's Word foreign, we will eventually feel alienated.
But when we acknowledge God, we will grow in knowledge of
Him and know Him better. When we seek to know His Word, we
will know our own worth.

The beautiful thing is, Gomer girl, because of Jesus, you will
never be "destroyed for lack of knowledge." When you *yada* Jesus,
you will know the truth that sets you free. When you have Jesus,
you have the wisdom of God at your fingertips, for Jesus Himself
is the very wisdom of God (see 1 Corinthians 1:30).

When You Have the Son, You Have Everything

There once lived a British widower who loved two things most
in life. He had just one child—a son—whom he loved dearly, and
he also loved to collect rare works of art. He owned all the grand
masters from Picasso to van Gogh. When Hitler attacked England,
the widower's son went off to war. Within a year the father was
notified that his son—whom he loved more than anyone or anything—had died courageously in battle. A few months later, while
the father was still grieving deeply, a young man about the age of
his son came to his home.

"Sir, you don't know me," said the young man as he handed a package to the widower, "but I served with your son in the war. He was carrying me to safety when he was struck, and he died instantly. He often talked about you and your love for art. I'm not much of an artist, but I wanted to do something to honor your son."

The father opened the package and found a portrait the young soldier had painted of his son. Although it was no great masterpiece, to the father it was a treasure, and it became his most prized possession. Whenever guests came to his home, he always showed the portrait of his son before showing them any of the other great works in his collection.

When the widower died, an auction of his paintings was scheduled. Art collectors from Europe and America gathered, excited for the chance to purchase one of his great paintings. The first painting brought to the front of the room and displayed on the platform was the young soldier's painting of the son.

The auctioneer pounded his gavel and announced, "We will start the bidding with this portrait of the son."

Silence echoed throughout the room.

"Who will make the first bid for this painting?" the auctioneer asked.

After a few more moments of silence, a voice called out, "We want to see the famous paintings! Please skip this one."

But the auctioneer persisted. "Will someone please open the bidding? One hundred dollars for the portrait of the son."

"We didn't come for this painting!" another voiced shouted angrily. "We came for the Rembrandt and the Michelangelo!"

Finally a voice came from the back of the room. The longtime gardener of the father, who had just stepped in, said, "I'll give ten dollars for the painting."

The auctioneer scanned the faces in the audience before saying, "We have ten dollars! Will anyone give me twenty dollars?"

The crowd was growing impatient. They hadn't come to bid on the picture of the son. They were after worthy investments for their collection.

The auctioneer pounded the gavel. "Going once, going twice...sold for ten dollars to the gentleman in the back!"

"Finally!" shouted one collector. "Now we can get on with the valuable paintings!"

"The auction is over," the auctioneer announced firmly as he laid down his gavel.

"What about the other paintings?" frantic voices shouted. "What about the Raphael? You must be kidding!"

"The will stipulated that only the painting of the son would be auctioned," replied the auctioneer, "and whoever bought that painting would inherit the entire collection."*

> When we have God's Son,
> we have everything.

It was the father's will that whoever took the portrait of the son would get everything, and that is the truth we will end our journey

---

* Robert J. Morgan, *Nelson's Complete Book of Stories, Illustrations & Quotes*, (Nashville: Thomas Nelson Publishers, 2000).

with, Gomer girl. When we have God's Son, we have everything! We have security. We have identity. We have value. We have satisfaction. When we know Jesus—when we *yada* Jesus—we have it all!

But if we ain't got *yada*, we ain't got nada!

Really! If we don't intimately know and love God, we have nothing. And we will lack everything—security, identity, purpose, a sense of our own value.

So as we end this book, let's turn to the next page of our lives and live like the beloved Gomer girls we are. Let's live with our identity in Christ instead of with an identity crisis. And if I get to heaven before you, I'll save you a seat so you, me, and Gomer can have coffee together and we can hear the rest of her story—which I hope has a very happy ending! I hope that she and Hosea grew old together and sat on their front porch watching their grandchildren play while the sun set behind the Judean hills.

And I think that if she could whisper something to us from wherever she is right now, she would whisper...

Keep pressing in and pressing on to know God.

Stay in His Word so you won't stray from His will.

Never forget that you are not how you feel.

Keep a right view of God, and you will have a right view of yourself.

Never overlook Truth, and you will never feel invisible.

And Gomer's final words to us may be identical to the final words I want to finish this book with for they are the final words from the book of Hosea.

Who is wise? Let them realize these things. Who is discerning? Let them understand. The ways of the LORD are right; the righteous walk in them, but the rebellious stumble in them.

Hosea 14:9

Well, Gomer girl, that's a wrap! Thank you for traveling this path of freedom with me. Please remember that God loves you and His love makes you lovely. Now, go be the beloved!

As I read
God's Word,
I see
my worth.

#TheInvisibleBook

Hosea in 1200 Words or Less

You may not have read the book of Hosea in the Old Testament before, so I would like to introduce it to you. The first few times I read Hosea, I was really confused! Part of it is Hosea's story, part of it is Gomer's story, and part of it is sermons Hosea preached to Israel. Some of it is poetry, some of it is prose, and most of it is confusing—until you know what you're reading!

To help you, I went through the book of Hosea and pulled several verses from each chapter to represent the heart of Hosea's message—and to make it easier for you to grasp. You can think of it as Hosea in 1200 words or less!

Now, there are a few things you need to know before reading this summary. First, the verses are not in chronological order. Second, Israel is also known as *Ephraim* in the book of Hosea, so whichever name you read—Israel or Ephraim—it's referring to the same people. In addition Gomer represents Israel, so the feminine pronouns are often used. Just remember that those—she, her, and so forth—refer to Israel too. Finally and most importantly, when you read this summary, please think of yourself when you read about Gomer and about Israel. Because you—like Gomer and Israel—are chosen, loved, and prone to wander, but you've also been forgiven and redeemed by your loving God.

When the LORD first spoke through Hosea, the LORD said to Hosea, "Go, take to yourself a wife of harlotry and have children of harlotry; for the land commits flagrant harlotry, forsaking the LORD.

My people consult a wooden idol,
   and a diviner's rod speaks to them.
A spirit of prostitution leads them astray;
   they are unfaithful to their God.
Moreover, the pride of Israel testifies against him,
And Israel and Ephraim stumble in their iniquity;
So my people are bent on turning from Me.
Though they (the prophets) call them to the One on high,
None at all exalts Him (Jehovah)
Ephraim is oppressed, crushed in judgment,
Because he was determined to follow man's command.
I wrote for them the many things of my law,
   but they regarded them as something foreign.
When I fed them, they were satisfied;
   when they were satisfied, they became proud;
      then they forgot me.
But they do not realize
   that I remember all their evil deeds.
Their sins engulf them;
   they are always before me.
I led them with cords of a man, with bonds of love,
And I became to them as one who lifts the yoke from their jaws;
And I bent down and fed them.
For she (Israel) does not know that it was I who gave her the grain, the new wine and the oil,
And lavished on her silver and gold which they used for Baal.

Yet it is I who taught Ephraim to walk,
I took them in My arms;
But they did not know that I healed them.
I trained them and strengthened their arms,
    but they plot evil against me.

When I found Israel,
    it was like finding grapes in the desert;
when I saw your ancestors,
    it was like seeing early fruit on the fig tree.
But when they came to Baal Peor,
    they consecrated themselves to that shameful idol
    and became as vile as the thing they loved.
But you have planted wickedness,
    you have reaped evil,
    you have eaten the fruit of deception.
Though Ephraim built many altars for sin offerings,
    these have become altars for sinning.
Because you have depended on your own strength
    and on your many warriors,
They do not turn to the Most High;
    they are like a faulty bow...
They sow the wind
    and reap the whirlwind.
You are destroyed, Israel,
    because you are against me, against your helper.
My people are destroyed from lack of knowledge.
Because you have rejected knowledge,
    I also reject you as my priests;
because you have ignored the law of your God,
    I also will ignore your children.

BUT...

How can I give you up, O Ephraim?
How can I surrender you, O Israel?
How can I make you like Admah?
How can I treat you like Zeboyim?
My heart is turned over within Me,
All My compassions are kindled.
I will not execute My fierce anger;
I will not destroy Ephraim again.
For I am God and not man, the Holy One in your midst,
And I will not come in wrath.
Therefore, behold, I will allure her (Israel),
Bring her into the wilderness
And speak kindly to her.
Then I will give her her vineyards from there.
And the valley of Achor as a door of hope.
I will heal their waywardness
   and love them freely,
     for my anger has turned away from them.
I will betroth you to Me forever;
Yes, I will betroth you to Me in righteousness and in justice,
In lovingkindness and in compassion,
And I will betroth you to Me in faithfulness.
Then you will know the LORD.

I will sow her for Myself in the land.
I will also have compassion on her who had not obtained
 compassion,
And I will say to those who were not My people,
"You are my people!"
And they will say, "You are my God!"

I will deliver this people from the power of the grave;
  I will redeem them from death.
Where, O death, are your plagues?
  Where, O grave, is your destruction?

SO...

The LORD said to me (Hosea), "Go, show your love to your wife again, though she is loved by another man and is an adulteress. Love her as the LORD loved the Israelites, though they turn to other gods and love the sacred raisin cakes."

So I bought her for fifteen shekels of silver and about a homer and a lethek of barley. Then I told her, "You are to live with me many days; you must not be a prostitute or be intimate with any man, and I will behave the same way toward you,"

I have been the LORD your God
  ever since you came out of Egypt.
You shall acknowledge no God but me,
  no Savior except me.

THEREFORE...

Return, Israel, to the LORD your God.
  Your sins have been your downfall!
But you must return to your God;
  maintain love and justice,
  and wait for your God always.
Sow righteousness for yourselves,
  reap the fruit of unfailing love,
and break up your unplowed ground;
  for it is time to seek the LORD,

until he comes
    and showers his righteousness on you.
Take words with you
    and return to the LORD.
Say to him:
    "Forgive all our sins
and receive us graciously,
    that we may offer the fruit of our lips.
Come, let us return to the LORD.
For He has torn us, but He will heal us;
He has wounded us, but He will bandage us."

Assyria cannot save us;
    we will not mount warhorses.
We will never again say "Our gods"
    to what our own hands have made,
    for in you the fatherless find compassion.

So let us know, let us press on to know the LORD.
His going forth is as certain as the dawn;
And He will come to us like the rain,
Like the spring rain watering the earth.

Who is wise? Let him realize these things. Who is discerning?
Let them understand. The ways of the Lord are right; the
righteous walk in them, but the rebellious stumble in them.

Let's keep in touch...

Thank you for letting me…and Gomer…be a part of your life. I pray God has used these words to strengthen, encourage, and challenge you to believe and live out the truth that you are not how you feel!

I'd love to hear from you—literally!

Did you know I have a computer that reads my email to me? I can't promise the digital voice sounds as nice as yours, but it does allow me to hear how God is working in your life and through this book. If you'd like to contact me, send an email to **JR@jenniferrothschild.com**, or better yet, go to the "contact us" link at **www.JenniferRothschild.com/Invisible**.

While you're there, sign up to receive Java with Jennifer. That way, we can stay connected over coffee every Friday! It's my blog that you'll get in your inbox. My hope is that I can pour some encouragement into your life and we can grow stronger and wiser from each other.

If you're on Facebook, find me at facebook.com/Jennifer.J.Rothschild.
If you tweet, I'm @jennrothschild.
On Instagram, you can locate me @jennrothschild.
And, of course, on Pinterest, I am jennrothschild.

And for those of you who actually still write letters—you know, with pen and paper, envelopes, and stamps—you can find me at:
4319 S. National Ave., Suite 303, Springfield, MO 65810

Well, Gomer Girl, you matter to me and you matter to God. I may be blind, but I can see your incredible beauty and value—I hope you see it too!

Love,

Jennifer

Other Great Resources from Jennifer Rothschild

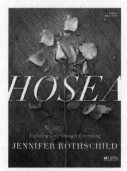

Hosea: Unfailing Love Changes Everything

In this 7-sesson DVD-driven study, you'll experience the love story of Hosea and Gomer; God and Israel. And, you'll discover it's your love story too! We're all like Gomer—deeply loved, but prone to wander—seeking acceptance and identity in all the wrong places. Through Hosea, Jennifer Rothschild will teach you how to know your God, know your identity, and live out your beautiful story.

Lessons I Learned in the Dark:
Steps to Walking by Faith, Not by Sight

At the age of fifteen, Jennifer Rothschild confronted two unshakable realities: Blindness is inevitable...and God is enough. Now this popular author, speaker, and recording artist offers poignant lessons that illuminate a path to freedom and fulfillment. With warmth, humor, and insight, Jennifer shares the guiding principles she walks by—and shows you how to walk forward by faith into God's marvelous light.

Me, Myself, and Lies:
A Thought Closet Makeover

Adapted from the trade book *Self Talk, Soul Talk*, in the Bible Study *Me, Myself and Lies* Jennifer shares practically and helpfully from her own life and from Scripture to show how every woman can turn her words—and her life—around for good.

This six-week Bible study for women encourages them to clean out the junk in their thoughts and replace these hidden negative thoughts and failures with positive truths from God's Word. Rather than struggling with self-esteem, body image, stress, and other unhealthy thoughts and emotions, they can learn to replace the lies they may have been telling themselves with the truth from God's Word.

www.JenniferRothschild.com

GIFTS FROM ME TO YOU

These cute little tools will help you remember that you
are never, ever invisible to God.

God's Love Compact Mirror

Every woman needs a mirror to check her hair, fix her lipstick, or see if she has broccoli between her teeth! But, Gomer Girl, we need to see more than flaws when we look in a mirror... we need to see the truth of who we are. This magnifying mirror is not only practical, but every time you see yourself in its reflection, it can remind you that you are not how you feel! As you see your beautiful face, you can tell yourself, "God loves me and His love makes me lovely" and "I am not the be-tolerated or the be-perfect, I am the beloved!" (Look in chapter 3 if you need to remember what to see in the mirror.)

Visit www.JenniferRothschild.com/Invisible and click on "Freebies" to place your order.
*Costs for shipping and handling will apply.
*Available only while supplies last.

Gomer Girl Manifesto

This is a must-have for me so I want you to have it too! Download and print this Gomer Girl Manifesto to proclaim the truth of who you are. You can send it to a friend, give it to your daughter, put it in your Bible, or on your mirror. I want you to have it because I want you to tuck these truths in your heart.

Visit www.JenniferRothschild.com/ Invisible and click on "Freebies" to download yours.

To learn more about Harvest House books and
to read sample chapters, visit our website:

www.harvesthousepublishers.com

HARVEST HOUSE PUBLISHERS
EUGENE, OREGON